COVER UP

Joan Freeman

Cover Up: Understanding Self-Harm

VERITAS

Published 2010 by
Veritas Publications
7–8 Lower Abbey Street
Dublin 1
Ireland

publications@veritas.ie
www.veritas.ie

ISBN 978-1-84730-212-0

10 9 8 7 6 5 4

A catalogue record for this book is available from the British Library.

Cover designed by Norma Prause-Brewer, Veritas Publications
Printed in Ireland by SPRINT-print Ltd, Dublin

Veritas books are printed on paper made from the wood pulp of managed forests. For every tree felled, at least one tree is planted, thereby renewing natural resources.

'They that sow in tears shall reap in joy' (Ps 126:5)

For Catherine

Acknowledgements

There are so many people to thank: my husband, Pat, who is the cornerstone of Pieta House and the cornerstone of my life; my Pieta House colleagues – wonderful, caring people who have supported me in every way possible; my sister Marian; my children, Marie, Siobhan, Aislinné and Martin; three special people who pushed and guided me before Pieta House even opened, Dr John Connolly, Barbara Cantwell and Deputy Dan Neville T.D.; and the selfless, gentle souls I have encountered here in Pieta House who have lost someone through suicide and in the midst of their sorrow have volunteered their time and efforts to prevent other families going through the same tragedy. Heartfelt thanks to the quiet, continuous support from ESB Electric Aid and the Arthur Guinness Fund who have brought Pieta House to the next level by allowing us to stand on their shoulders.

'There are persons so radiant, so genial, so kind, so pleasure-bearing, that you instinctively feel in their presence that they do you good, whose coming into a room is like the bringing of a lamp there.'

Henry Ward Beecher

Contents

Introduction

Life is extraordinary! You can be going around doing the usual things: cleaning the house, working, collecting the children from school, cooking, more cleaning, more working. Then something happens, and your life is never the same again. If someone had told me seven years ago that I would be running a centre that counsels people who self-harm or are suicidal, with nearly thirty staff, as well as writing a book about it, I would never have believed them – but it is true!

My background in psychology started with undertaking study during the years I was at home rearing my children. By the time they started school I was qualified to begin working as a counsellor and therapist. It was while working as a counsellor in a private practice that I experienced the loss of a loved one through suicide. In my work I had met only a few people who were suicidal and my attitude had been, if they were serious about suicide, they would not be talking about it – rather they would have done it by now. How ignorant of me. I had absolutely no understanding of suicide. Worse than that, I had absolutely no compassion. My ignorance led me to assume that people who have attempted suicide or behave in a self-harming way are dysfunctional and have psychiatric problems that can only be dealt with through medication and hospitalisation. That was until the tragedy of suicide came to my door.

When this happened, I was catapulted into a world of great sadness, but more so into a world of enormous anger. This anger was directed at everyone, but especially towards myself. I couldn't explain why I was angry. However, I did not feel any anger towards the person who had died, just terrible sorrow and shame because I had let her down – I didn't save her.

Very shortly after the tragedy, I began to go to the local library every day. We did not have the internet at home at the time, so I would book time on the computer and trawl through internet sites on suicide. I became like a scavenger, collecting as many bits of information as possible that mentioned suicide. I suddenly realised what I was doing: I was looking for answers. I was asking 'Why?' – why had this happened?

I remember not having the energy or the desire to get up, get dressed or even to survive, and I took to my bed. Surrounded by books, I came across one given to me by a nun – *The Seven Sorrows of Mary*. As I glanced through it, I came across a chapter that dealt with Mary's sorrow over the death of her son. At the start of this chapter was a reproduction of the famous Pietà sculpture by Michelangelo. This beautiful statue is of the Madonna holding the body of her dead son, Jesus. Michelangelo intentionally made Mary's body larger than her son's: her shoulders are broad and her lap deep so that she can hold, embrace and accept the broken body of Jesus. She looks outwards to her world, not in an accusatory way or in anger, but with enormous compassion. '*Pietà*', the Italian word for 'mercy', comes from the Latin '*pietās*', which means 'compassion'.

That day, lying in bed, the desire to care for people who were suicidal emerged. I didn't know what it was I was going to do, or how I was going to do it, but I knew I had to do something. The image of the Pietà stayed very firmly in my head. This universally recognised sculpture could become the symbol of compassion and understanding for people who were contemplating taking their lives or for those who had already attempted it. For me, this sculpture did not represent something strictly religious; rather, it represented the essence of compassion. I wanted to create an organisation that would hold, embrace and accept the broken lives of people. Thus, Pieta House was born.

Pieta House, set up in 2006, was the first centre in Ireland that specialised in the prevention of self-harm and suicide. Pieta is an alternative way of helping people in crisis, but it is also a way that encourages collaboration with hospitals and doctors.

We are all born with an innate desire to survive. As humans our instinct is to live and avoid pain, and our struggle is mainly about self-preservation. That is why suicide and self-harm seem not only terrifying but also inexplicable. It is probably why both are rarely spoken about. Suicide is still a taboo subject, while self-harm is normally consigned to sensationalist storylines on melodramas or labelled as being the eccentric behaviour of some celebrities. On top of that, there has never been any focused attention paid to it or any focused therapy created for the behaviour.

Before Pieta, people who were suicidal would often end up either in hospital, in a psychiatric unit or heavily medicated – sometimes all three. In many cases, patients were put on 'suicide watch', a procedure that involves the patient being watched by a nurse or carer every moment of every day – even while having showers or using the toilet. In some cases, this was the only way to guarantee the patient's safety – there was no alternative, and whether we liked the practice or not, lives were saved. However, we were convinced that there had to be some other way of helping people who were suicidal.

Prior to my own personal experience of suicide, other therapists and I were guilty of fuelling the notion that a person who is suicidal is 'unwell' or 'sick', and very quickly, on hearing that someone was in crisis, we would send them to their GP. However, in many cases the workload of GPs is huge and they are stretched way beyond their means. They are doctor, psychiatrist, nurse and therapist rolled into one, and other than listening to the patient and prescribing medication, they are limited in what they can do. We see the same thing in our Accident and Emergency departments: over-worked staff in crisis mode, having to make judgement calls and prioritise cases. People who self-harm or are suicidal often endure long waiting times before they are seen and then, once they have been assessed, they are usually referred to their local health centre and sent home. This is not because of a lack of care, but rather a lack of psychiatric facilities.

Just as physical ailments need specific treatments, I believe suicide and self-harm also need specific treatments, in particular a therapy that deals exclusively with people who are in despair and who find it difficult to cope with life events. Many therapists deal with general issues and there are several therapeutic approaches that are excellent for problems such as relationship breakdown and bereavement, as well as treatments that involve cognitive therapy to help people manage, for example, obsessive compulsive disorder or phobias. However, when dealing with self-harm and suicide, the most appropriate action initially is short-term crisis intervention, followed by therapy that focuses on the present and encourages the person to look forward to the future, rather than reflecting on the past and its problems.

When I question the reasoning behind my speedy GP referrals in the past, I can see that this action was based on fear – my fear. What if this person dies while they are attending me? What if I can't save them? What if I say the wrong thing? In fact, my fear sent out the very strong message that this suicidal person in front of me could not be helped. My fear reinforced their fear and stopped me from realising a very important fact, which is that most suicides are preventable.

While I truly believe this, I also know that there are some people who cannot be saved. Many therapists/psychiatrists will be bereaved through client/patient suicides each year. Most of them will have done everything possible to help the distressed person. They, too, need to grieve and mourn, and in the end they will come to accept the decision of their client. Ultimately, we cannot be responsible for the decision or actions of others, but we must also accept that suicide prevention is everyone's business.

When Pieta House opened I thought that we would be dealing with people with long-term depression who were suicidal. I was wrong. The people who come to us mainly fall into two groups: suicidal people who are reacting to a life event, and people who self-harm. The journey into this discovery has been an incredible one.

We have discovered at Pieta House that more times than not, self-harm has nothing to do with suicide; they are two very different behaviours. However, the little we knew about suicide, we discovered we knew even less about self-harm. And so, heretofore, self-harm had been lumped in with other suicidal behaviours.

Self-harming is a behaviour that can be found in young and old alike. However, this book will focus on understanding self-harm in relation to the young person who undertakes this behaviour. In the following chapters, I will explain what self-harm is, why a child might self-harm and, more importantly, what we can do to help. This book is for every parent, teacher, therapist or person in the medical profession who deals with young people who self-harm. For parents especially, I hope this book will remove any fear you may have if you discover that your child self-harms. This book is not a vehicle or a forum to criticise the parenting skills of people whose children self-harm; rather it is a book that can give you an insight into why your child self-harms. I believe that this book will help you examine and identify new ways in which you can communicate with your child and, more importantly, how your child is trying to communicate with you.

Ultimately, it is my hope that this book fosters a more compassionate understanding of self-harm and suicide and a more hopeful view that we can all turn tragic situations into positive actions.

Chapter One
Understanding Self-Harm by Understanding Suicide

This chapter will deal specifically with suicide. It will discuss why there is such a stigma attached to it, and will identify and dispel the many falsehoods that surround suicide by looking at the facts.

It will then go on to deal with the reasons why someone would choose to die by suicide, focusing on the issues and problems that concern specific ages, from the child right through to the older person.

The overall purpose of this chapter is to inform and educate about the warning signs of suicide and what to do if you discover that someone you know or love is suicidal.

Although I have kept suicide specifically to this one chapter, the subject will be referred to throughout the book, regarding in particular how it might be, in certain situations, linked to self-harm.

Suicide Throughout History
Suicide has been around for a very long time. It was written about in the Bible, when Judas Iscariot hanged himself after he betrayed Jesus, his friend and master, to the Roman soldiers. Samson pulled down the pillars

of the temple with the words, 'Let me die with the Philistines', thus killing himself and many others. In early Christianity, suicide was strongly appealing. This was probably because the act was often seen to be one of martyrdom. The most notable group who were enthusiastic in their promotion and encouragement of suicide was the Donatists, who believed that by killing themselves they would have a direct path to heaven. This was not only tolerated by the Church, but was actively condoned.

In the sixth century, the Church changed tack and decided to promote teachings of the immorality of suicide. Those who had taken their own lives were denied a Christian burial. If someone even attempted suicide they were regarded as having committed an ecclesiastical crime; this person would then be excommunicated.

It was not just the Church who tried to prevent further deaths by suicide. In later centuries, civil and criminal laws were imposed to discourage suicide. This resulted in the person not only being denied a proper burial, but also the confiscation of the possessions of the deceased and their family.

Today, suicide is viewed differently, though there is still much shame and taboo attached to the act. In 1993, suicide was decriminalised by the State, while the Church also changed its attitude, with burial being permitted in sacred grounds and the acknowledgement that the person who died by suicide did so with a mind that was distraught and unable to make rational decisions.

The Myths of Suicide

There are many untruths surrounding suicide. Many people believe that if a person talks about suicide they won't take their lives, or that most suicides occur with no warning. The complete opposite is true.

People who talk about suicide are obviously feeling suicidal. They may make clear statements such as, 'I don't want to live anymore', 'I see no future', 'I want to die', or, 'I don't see the point of my life anymore'. Or they may ask questions like, 'Would you miss me/be alright/be better off without me?'

Certain behaviours can also provide signs. For example, a person might begin to give away their possessions, or they might make a will. One of the most obvious signs – but one that is sadly often missed – is when a person purchases a rope or other paraphernalia that could aid in bringing about their death.

Many people at some stage in their life think about suicide. At Pieta House, we have discovered that it is not necessarily those who are seriously depressed or who suffer psychiatric disorders that end up attempting suicide or having suicidal ideation: it can be anyone – it could be you or me. We have discovered that suicide can follow a serious life event that leaves the person reeling. Take, for example, the couple who have been together for a few years and have two children. Suddenly, they end their relationship. The woman remains in the family home with the children. The man leaves and, within a few weeks, is either contemplating suicide or attempting suicide. Why is this? I believe the reasons are loss and isolation. This man has not only lost a romantic relationship but also his home, more than likely a shared circle of friends and, in many cases, spontaneous access to his children. In other words, overnight this person has lost everything, and this loss is so huge that he cannot see his way through the pain or come up with a solution that will ease his problem. The only alternative this person sees is to take his life.

Take, for example, a woman in her fifties (suicide in women in their fifties is the highest rate amongst women in Ireland (National Suicide Research Foundation, 2009)). Look at what could be happening in her life. Chances are that her children are now grown up and have left home, so her identity as a mother has suddenly gone. Maybe her relationship has suffered because she has devoted her life to her children. Many women of this age feel invisible. On top of all that, they are more than likely going through the menopause, which signifies an end to their fertility and their femininity as they know it. So many pieces of identity have been chipped away.

Media in the past have highlighted the rate of suicides amongst young males between the ages of seventeen and twenty-four, which may lead people to believe that we should only concentrate on young men. Studies do tell us that the number of young men who take their lives in Ireland is higher than in any other country in the European Union. In Ireland, our research shows that the second highest risk group, after young men, is men aged between forty and forty-four, followed closely by men aged forty-five to fifty-four. However, it is important to remember that these studies only tell part of the story. Suicide affects every age and gender. If we stay focused on one group, we will miss the opportunity to recognise problems in another. We are all vulnerable at different stages in our lives – all age groups and both genders are at risk. The youngest person we encountered in Pieta House was seven; the oldest was seventy-five. Suicide knows no boundaries; it does not discriminate based on age, gender or class.

Another myth about suicide is that the lethality of the attempt indicates the seriousness of the intent. This myth peddles the notion that if, for example, someone uses a gun or rope, they are more serious about suicide than those who overdose. This is simply not true: people will use methods that they are more comfortable with or have to hand. The person who takes an overdose may have the same intention to die as the person who uses a rope; the only difference is that a rope is, more often than not, lethal, while with an overdose there is a chance of survival.

Finally, one myth that should be blown out of the water is that suicidal people want to die. The truth is that people who are suicidal are quite ambivalent about life and death. Most people do not want to die – they just want to end their suffering, and while sleep may give them some relief from their despairing thoughts, the irrational belief is that only death will end their pain for good; they see no alternative. Someone once described to me what it was like to be suicidal: 'Imagine you are all alone at the top of a very tall building, and it's engulfed in flames – the only escape is to jump!'

Facts About Suicide
- Although there is an impulsive element to many suicides, it is mainly seen as the only option when there are no other alternatives.

- Suicide is not a cry for help, it is an act to end unendurable pain.
- Only about one-third of people leave notes; more often nowadays these are in the form of text messages or emails.
- If someone dies by suicide on a significant day (Christmas or someone's birthday) or in a significant place, it is not out of malice that the person has chosen that day or that place, but because they want to be remembered or included on that significant day or in that significant place.
- It is thought that if a person returns to a significant place in their past, such as the house they grew up in or a place where they spent holidays, they are hoping that the people who are left behind will remember them when they were happy and when life was good.

The Seven Vulnerable Stages of Being Human

We need to be aware who is at risk, and we need to know what warning signs to look for. Always listen to someone when they express suicidal thoughts, and believe that if someone expresses that they are feeling suicidal, it is better to err on the side of caution than to blithely disregard the threat.

Who is at risk? As mentioned before, everyone is at risk: everyone who has ever experienced a serious life event, who has little or no support, or who is unable to look for help and support. There are also certain times in our lives when, due to age or circumstances, we are more vulnerable. I call these the Seven Vulnerable Stages of Being Human.

Eleven Years and Under

Thankfully, there are very few children in Ireland who die by suicide. The children who have come to us and have disclosed that they feel suicidal are usually intelligent, articulate children who use the word in the appropriate context. This could mean one of two things: that they are so intelligent, they understand and can visualise suicide; or they have heard of suicide (a neighbour, family friend or relative may have died by suicide) and use the concept of suicide as a way to express or communicate their distress over some event – they may not mean it the first time, but it could become a viable option for them.

What would cause a child to feel so distressed that they would rather be dead? At this stage of a child's life, their self-esteem, confidence and belief in themselves is based on the opinion of the adults in their lives. Although they get distressed if they are ignored or bullied in school, what happens after school, in their home life or in extracurricular activities can compensate for what is missing in their school life. In particular, their parents' and teachers' opinions matter. These are the people who will tell them they are loveable, clever, kind and so on, but they may also tell them they are bold, selfish and lazy. Almost all children can survive and thrive on this type of parenting, but there are some children who are so sensitive to any criticism, so easily bruised psychologically, that they are damaged by it. Suicide in this situation can be an impulsive or knee-jerk reaction to remarks that might not even register with other children. This knee-jerk reaction can take place if the child has recently been made aware of the circumstances of another suicide, especially if it is someone they know and can identify with.

Twelve–Sixteen Years

These are such delicate, vulnerable years for the developing teenager. There are so many changes in their life – the commencement of secondary school, physical and emotional development, heightened emphasis in the expectations of teachers and parents, peer scrutiny.

At this stage of a child's development, they need recognition and approval from those their own age for their well-being and self-esteem. Previously, it only mattered how their parents thought or felt about them; now the young person's confidence or lack thereof is dependent on the opinions and attitudes of their peers. The popular nursery rhyme, 'Sticks and stones may break my bones but names will never hurt me', is unfortunately not applicable to children this age. A young person who is searching for their identity relies heavily on the labels their peers place on them. Therefore, whatever name or label is attached to a person now will influence how they see themselves.

Bullying and social exclusion are rampant during this stage of development. The experience of bullying is most traumatic and damaging. Whatever you have experienced at this stage in your life, whatever your opinion of yourself, tends to stay with you for many years, sometimes always. When young people of this age come to us at Pieta House after a suicide attempt, they usually disclose that this is not their first attempt. What is worrying is that if they are not helped at this time, it could be the start of a pattern of suicidal behaviours that could last for many years or until suicide is completed. Young people really believe they are invincible, and so a suicide attempt is often a reaction to a given moment or distressing situation. The fear is that our young people do not fully comprehend the finality or the fatality of suicide.

SIXTEEN–TWENTY-FOUR YEARS

This age group is the most cited by researchers and the media because more young men in this age bracket in Ireland die by suicide (with our country having the fifth highest rate of suicide in Europe) than in any other age bracket. The reasons behind this are many and varied and, in most situations, complicated. We need to consider the kinds of situation people of this age may be facing.

At this age, young men can experience conflict in relationships, and often the ending of relationships; they may abuse alcohol or drugs; for some young men, a lack of focus or structure in their lives, often a result of unemployment, little or no interaction with other male friends, or being in a high-risk environment where suicide is a regular occurrence, can contribute to the development of suicidal thoughts.

For young women in this age group, issues such as poor body image, poor self-esteem, conflict in or ending of relationships and isolation due to early motherhood can lead to thoughts of suicide.

Sexual orientation and isolation or discrimination arising from it in both this and the previous age group can also be distressing and a causal factor of suicide.

TWENTY-FOUR–FORTY YEARS

Studies indicate that suicidal ideation levels off during this time in a person's life. People have stronger reasons for living, for staying alive: the arrival of children, supportive and loving relationships, gratifying and satisfying employment, a healthy and supportive network of friends and family.

However, if this stabilising and life-enhancing dynamic begins to unravel or disappear, then suicide can become a consideration for some. As mentioned previously, when a relationship ends, men in particular find the sense of loss enormous, simply because all those life-sustaining factors vanish almost overnight.

In contrast, for women it is being single – not due to separation or divorce but rather because of lack of or missed opportunities, causing them to feel unloved, isolated and lonely. The possibility of not having children could also cause women to feel great despair.

It would appear that the fundamental cause of suicidal ideation in both men and women of this age group is a sense of failure – a failure at life, or at the common understanding of what constitutes a success-ful, fully-rounded life.

Forty–Fifty-Five Years
Men and women in this age group can experience an overwhelming sense of loss at this stage of their life. For women, there is the aforementioned loss of their femininity, fertility and identity as a mother. They also often find themselves caring for their elderly parents. Men of this age can feel a sense of loss, especially those who have never married. They may look back and wonder what they have to show for their life. There is also a great sense of loneliness, particularly amongst men in rural areas and those who are living alone after separation or divorce.

FIFTY-FIVE–SEVENTY YEARS

People in this age group may experience a sense of loss and loneliness with children moving away; they may have lost their youthful mobility and might now be experiencing a marked reduction in energy. Retirement might be enforced, either due to statutory age regulations or because of physical ability. They may encounter ageism and notice a loss of respect towards them, when wisdom and experience is seen as neither an attribute nor a resource.

SEVENTY+

This is a period of great physical and mental change. Facing mortality – that of oneself and of others – is probably the main concern of this age group. It is the time of losing partners, family and friends, as well as the ability to do even the simplest things, such as drive a car or go up the stairs unaided. It is a time of increased dependency and of giving up one's dignity in circumstances where physical help is needed. It can also be a time for regrets and for ruminating on what could have or should have been.

Most of us pass through these seven stages with little difficulty. We can cope with whatever life throws at us, and while certain stages can be difficult, we are usually fortunate enough to have people in our lives that support and encourage us through distressing or traumatic events. The people who do not get through these difficult times often have nobody in their lives, or believe they have nobody in their lives to whom they can turn.

Now I will look at some of the warning signs that indicate when someone is at risk:

- Changes in the usual pattern of living. For example, the person who stops performing well in school, begins to miss days at work, doesn't keep the house clean or stops paying attention to their personal hygiene.
- Changes in normal physical patterns. For example, someone who usually sleeps well begins to have trouble sleeping and is now awake for several hours during the night; or perhaps they are sleeping more than usual but still wake up feeling exhausted.
- Someone's eating patterns might change. For example, they may either comfort eat or skip meals because of lack of appetite.
- Activity levels drop. For example, someone who is normally very active now spends hours doing little or nothing. Perhaps an everyday activity (such as collecting the children from school or going to work) now seems to demand huge amounts of energy. Likewise, activities that someone used to consider enjoyable, such as walking, gardening or playing football, are now considered a chore, requiring energy that they don't have.
- Self-enforced isolation. For example, a person who is normally sociable, talkative and involved is now withdrawn and has ceased normal social activities. They might also go to bed too early, retreating to their bedroom. They might not answer the phone or the door or they might turn their mobile phone off.
- Religious despair. Expressing the feeling that they have been abandoned by God or that there is no God.

- Other warning signs include an interest in morbid music or poetry; looking up internet sites that contain morbid or dark information on death or suicide; talking about death or how pointless life is; writing funeral plans; making out a will; or, in what has become a worrying trend, posting or sending messages revealing a distressed state to friends and acquaintances on social networking sites.

Using Family, Friends and the Community as a Resource in the Fight Against Suicide

As mentioned earlier, many therapists are afraid of having a client who may be suicidal, so imagine how a family member feels if they are confronted by someone in crisis. If they take the person seriously, and believe that they are thinking of ending their lives, the fear can be unbearable. However, if they don't take the threat seriously, the situation might not be given its due consideration. Those well-meaning statements such as 'pull yourself together', 'snap out of it', or, 'it's just a phase' are made, I believe, not as reassuring words for the person who is in crisis, but as reassurance for those dealing with the suicidal person.

It is family, friends, colleagues or neighbours who may be able to identify if someone is at risk. No matter how many Pieta Houses are set up around the country, someone has to first identify the person who is at risk, and that someone could be you.

I firmly believe that suicide is a problem that affects the whole community; we need to remove the stigma surrounding suicide, suicidal behaviour and mental illness so that if someone is in trouble, friends, family and neighbours will feel able to rally around to help.

I often tell the story about how my grandparents had an arranged marriage. The day my grandfather took his new bride to his home, she must have thought she had done very well for herself. The kitchen fire was blazing while a pot of stew was gently cooking over it. The chairs had plump cushions resting on them, the dishes on the dresser shone in the bright firelight, and in the bedroom the double bed had crisp white sheets turned down. The newness of her situation must have been softened for my grandmother when she saw all these lovely things in her new home. Can you imagine then how she felt when, first thing the next morning, all the neighbours arrived, one taking away the cushions, the other taking away the dishes and, most humiliating of all, another neighbour whipping the sheets off the bed? The items had been lent out for my grandmother's first day in her marital home.

While this must have been quite embarrassing for her, it also showed the kindness and compassion of her neighbours. They tried not only to make her feel welcome, but also to make this new life a bit easier for the young bride. I think for many of us, it's hard to imagine having supportive neighbours and friends like that, but for us to tackle suicide seriously, we need to come back to that supportive, caring community we used to be. We are very quick to blame the government when the numbers of people who die by suicide increase. But think for a moment: if your loved one was in crisis, who would you ring, a government minister or your neighbour?

However, for you to be able to recognise signs of suicide, you need to educate yourself about the subject. So let's get this straight once and for all: the reason behind the act of suicide is to end negative and painful thoughts that seem to the person unendurable and unending, without any possible solution. The act is self-inflicted and is not the result of another person's action or behaviour. A person does not 'commit' suicide, because suicide is neither a criminal act nor a sin. It is without a doubt an unnecessary end to a very necessary life – a death that could be prevented, a life that could be prolonged if only we knew how.

What To Do if Someone is Suicidal
There are signs that clearly indicate when someone is distressed. If there is a combination of these signs, then this person is in crisis. The secret is to be aware, be alert and be not afraid to ask.

Now that you know who is potentially at risk and what signs to look out for, what do you do with all this information and, more importantly, what do you do if you discover someone is suicidal? The answer is APR: Ask Persuade Refer – the emotional resuscitation of someone who is in emotional crisis.

ASK. If you are concerned about someone's emotional well-being or if you feel that you recognise the signs of someone in crisis, don't be afraid to ask, 'Are you suicidal?' If they are suicidal, they will answer you truthfully – that is, if they feel safe with you, if they trust that they won't be stigmatised or hospitalised. They will be relieved that someone notices and is not afraid to ask the question that has been filling them with such fear. If they are not suicidal, they will simply say 'No' and may perhaps ask you why you felt it necessary to ask that question. This gives you a wonderful opportunity to make them aware that you care about them and that their behaviour has seemed different lately. Do not underestimate the power of such a simple question. As stated before, it is far better to query and risk seeming overly cautious about the perceived mood and intentions of someone else than to ignore them entirely.

PERSUADE. If the person has said that they are suicidal, what do you do? First, try to persuade this person to allow you to get help for them. It is no good trying to convince them to go and get help – they weren't able to do that before, so why would they find it easier now? Tell them that you are going to be involved and that you and other people will help them through this. Persuade them to give this a try, to trust you; tell them they have nothing to lose.

Second, make plans. Start by gathering an army of people who will support and help you with this situation. Inform family, friends, relatives – anyone who can help you make sure that this person stays safe. It is very important that someone who is suicidal is not left alone, as this gives them the opportunity to brood and ruminate. It is also important that you have other people involved because the responsibility of this person's life could overwhelm you. You need to share this; you need your own self-care. Further, having more people on board will reinforce to the person in crisis how important and loved they are and how concerned everyone is for their welfare. I have seen cases where families and friends flock around a person who is in crisis to the point that they even sleep with them at night time to ensure that they are not left alone.

REFER. The emotional energy and loving support of family and friends is incredibly powerful – but it has a life span. During this time of cocooning it would be very easy to allow the urgency of the situation to dissipate, so it is at this time that you need to get professional help.

Whether it is somewhere like Pieta House or another organisation that offers crisis intervention, make sure that the person attends and that it is the right sort of intervention. Do not be afraid to ask for second opinions; gather as much information as possible.

It is essential that the person in crisis is not forced to face the failings or negative events in their life (whether real or imaginary). What is required is a practical, solution-focused approach to the problems facing them at present and gentle reminders of what has worked and is good in their life. It is also essential that this professional help is not once a week or fortnightly, but rather every couple of days, or in some cases daily, so that the momentum is not lost and the despair not allowed to creep back in. However, remember that professional help usually lasts just one hour, so, even if it takes place daily, what happens during the other twenty-three hours? This is why you must have an army of people ready to help the distressed person. Crisis has a short life span. With the right support – personal and professional – not only will a person be able to get through this, but they will also learn new skills that will help them cope with future difficulties.

I have focused on suicide in this chapter so that the differences between it and self-harm will become clear. Getting it right could save a person from ending their life or help a person cope with their life. However, it is important to note that self-harm usually starts in childhood, while suicidal ideation at this age is unlikely.

However, if self-harm is allowed to continue and goes unnoticed or unchecked, over a period of years the person can move from using self-harming as a way of coping to considering suicide as the only way out of despair. A history of self-harming often prefigures a suicide attempt. We must also acknowledge that strong emotions do not always follow the usual solutions for people who self-harm. Sometimes a person can be so distressed that the thought of self-harm is not enough at that moment, that to end it all is considered the only solution. In a recent survey in Northern Ireland, adolescents were questioned about their self-harming behaviours and when asked what their reasons for self-harming were, in both girls and boys the second most common answer was: 'to die' (with the most common being 'to communicate').

Although in Pieta House we stand by our conviction that suicide and self-harm are two very different behaviours that have very different functions, we are aware that once a person is on a path of dangerous behaviours, it might only be a matter of time before someone reaches the end of the line.

The next chapter will look at what self-harm really is and consider it from the perspective of parents or carers.

Chapter Two
What is Self-Harm?

Imagine, as a parent, that you have just walked into your child's bedroom to find them sitting on the bed, their sleeve rolled up, with long, thin cuts exposed, blood trickling from them. Time seems to stand still. You are confused – what is happening? What are you feeling? Anger, shame, disgust, pity, compassion or disbelief? Maybe all of them.

Or imagine you and your child have gone swimming and you suddenly notice that there are marks on their arms and thighs. When you question them, they tell you that they fell, that it's nothing. But you seem to remember seeing these marks before and being told the same thing – it's nothing!

You are waiting in Accident and Emergency for the third time this year. Once again your son has a broken bone – his wrist/arm/foot. He seems to be always getting into fights, and is so accident-prone; just the other day he fell down the stairs. Yet he never complains; he never cries or shows that he is in pain. Over the years you have brought him to hospital twenty-nine times with a broken or smashed something or other. What's wrong with him?

Mary is only sixteen, but this is her fourth overdose. She swore she didn't attempt suicide and can't understand why no one believes her.

Self-harm can be called many things: self-injury, self-mutilation or even self-abuse. Self-harm or deliberate self-harm, which includes self-injuring and self-poisoning, is the intentional injuring of body tissue without, in most cases, suicidal intent. Self-harm behaviour is very often lumped in with suicide. However, most of those who participate in self-harming behaviours will tell you that suicide is the furthest thing from their mind. This kind of behaviour is usually hidden and is far more widespread than people realise. I often ask people how they knew to self-harm, why did they think that self-harm would help them in any way? For many people, they had heard of self-harm through television programmes or teenage magazines; for others, the thought and the action came naturally. For those who tried to self-harm simply out of curiosity, the pain of the action stopped them very quickly.

Examples of Self-Harm

To the uninformed, the image of someone self-harming is of a person impulsively and frenetically cutting and slashing at themselves, when in fact for most young people the opposite is true. Self-harm can be a ritualistic process that is carried out with great precision; making cuts that are a certain length and depth, for example. It is this repetitive and familiar behaviour that can, for a short period, make the person feel in control and soothed at the same time. Self-harm involves a spectrum of behaviours, not alone self-cutting. Listed below are different behaviours:

Binge drinking	Extreme exercising
Smoking	Workaholism
Body piercing	Biting
Burning	Hitting
Sexual promiscuity	Scratching
Inserting or swallowing	Asphyxiation
objects	Physical inactivity
Picking or gouging	Head banging
Nail biting	Bingeing and purging
Substance misuse	Food restriction
Body tattooing	Obesity

Are you surprised with this list? People might not consider many of these behaviours to be self-harm, such as binge drinking or food restriction, yet this is what they are.

There are two main differences between self-harming manifested as binge drinking or food restriction, and as cutting or burning:

- Whereas the results of cutting or burning are immediate, obvious and visible, bingeing and food restriction are harmful to the body over a long period of time.
- Smoking, binge drinking or food restriction are all more or less socially acceptable.

In reality we all self-harm to some degree and we do it for many reasons. For example, food restricting could be because of poor body image; binge drinking could be as a result of poor self-esteem or lack of confidence; nail biting could be as a result of an underlying anxiety. All harmful behaviours have a function.

Most of the behaviours listed above are 'adult'-type behaviours, although studies show that more and more children are drinking, smoking and engaging in sexual behaviour. However, this book will focus on the more extreme types of self-harm, from those that can be life-threatening and may necessitate medical attention (such as cutting or ingestion of tablets), to those that are more superficial and do not require outside help (such as hitting or head banging). I will also talk in brief about self-harm and eating disorders.

There are many self-harming behaviours that, from a parent's point of view, go undetected.

- Nail picking/biting: picking begins at the side of the nail bed rather than the usual top part of the nail; in the extreme, this causes fingers to bleed.
- Hair pulling: this behaviour, called trichotil-lomania, is often confused with alopecia (which is hereditary, though often exacerbated by stress). It is when a child pulls or plucks their hair from either their scalp or their eyelashes and eye-brows. Permanent damage to hair follicles and unwanted peer attention could result from this behaviour.
- Body bashing: this involves people throwing themselves down stairs or against walls, or hitting themselves in the face and breaking their bones. This type of self-harm is the most undetected, as injuries are usually mistaken for accidents, either at home or in school. This sort of behaviour can be accepted as a sports injury, with boys in particular, or a 'harmless fight' between two lads. And while fights are often

instigated so that a boy who self-harms can feel pain, more often than not these types of injuries are self-inflicted.

- Insertion/ingestion of objects: this behaviour, particularly the insertion of objects, seems to occur in those over twenty years of age. Ingested objects could vary from teaspoons to batteries to bleach or other cleaning liquids. This type of behaviour is particularly distressing. The obvious dangers are, of course, choking and poisoning, and when objects have to be surgically removed there are the usual dangers of anaesthetic or post-operative complications.
- Burning: this type of self-harming could be mistaken as an accident. Getting burned by an iron or a cooker or being scalded by boiling water can happen to anyone. However, if it is a regular occurrence or if the wound doesn't seem to be healing (due to the person picking at it), then this is not an accident. The dangers of this type of self-harm are infection and disfigurement.
- Asphyxiation: this involves holding one's breath, placing a bag over one's head or tying a scarf/belt around one's neck. Although this behaviour would only last for a short while, the obvious danger is that if the person passes out, brain damage or death could occur. This could be misinterpreted as a suicide attempt.
- Cutting: this behaviour is probably the one that most people associate with self-harm and is indeed the most common. It usually starts off at an early age as scratching, either with the finger-nail or the point of a pin, scissors or compass. It

can progress to cutting with broken glass and then later with blades. The danger here is that a main artery could be severed by accident.

Some of the behaviours that have been described are extreme, but they do happen, usually after a long time of emotional neglect, where the person's emotional pain has gone unnoticed or been ignored. It is essential that we realise that all self-harming behaviours are progressive, both physically and emotionally. That is why I firmly believe that if we can spot distress that leads to self-harming behaviours in early childhood, we can prevent a lifetime of body disfigurement, poor coping skills and a distressed state of mind.

The Myths About Self-Harm

Let's explore some of the myths that are attached to self-harming behaviours.

SELF-HARM IS A SUICIDE ATTEMPT

This is a common myth and something that needs to be clarified. In the early stages in particular, most self-harming is superficial; in other words, it does not cause life-threatening injuries. Later on in the book I will discuss how children who embark on a life of self-harm are attempting in their own way to cope with an emotion or situation. At this stage they do not see this behaviour as a way of ending their life.

SELF-HARM IS ATTENTION SEEKING

This statement is widely used and abused. Self-harm is one of the most hidden behaviours and is often only discovered by accident. If someone does display their wounds, then their 'attention seeking' is actually 'attention needing'. They are trying to tell us that there is something wrong.

PEOPLE WHO SELF-HARM DO NOT FEEL ANY PAIN
This is partially true: at the time of hurting themselves, people who self-harm may not feel pain, but they will suffer the consequences of their injuries later.

This can also be said about people who participate in sport: for example, in rugby it is not until the game is over that many players feel the cuts and bruises that they acquired. This is because they are so involved in their game that their wounds go unnoticed. The immediate pain of people who self-harm also goes unnoticed because they are immersed in their emotional distress.

PEOPLE WHO SELF-HARM HAVE A MENTAL DISORDER
As you work your way through this book you will come to realise that people who self-harm are not mad, disturbed or crazy – just very distressed. You would be surprised at the people who self-harm, particularly adults who on the outside appear calm, successful and 'together'.

PEOPLE WHO SELF-HARM MUST HAVE A VIOLENT NATURE AND COULD BE A DANGER TO OTHERS
This could not be further from the truth. In Pieta House we have found that people who self-harm are sensitive, gentle people who are easily bruised emotionally and would rather hurt themselves than hurt anyone else.

SELF-HARM IS ADDICTIVE

This statement is not only misleading but also dangerous. It is so easy to label different behaviours and put them into a category that suggests that the 'fault' of the behaviour lies in the area of addiction or the person who is too lazy to change their behaviour. It may look like an addiction or a habit, but people hurt themselves because this is the only way they know how to express their distress or to cope with the particular strong emotion that they are feeling at that time.

The Facts of Self-Harm

Now that we have blown away those myths, let's look at some of the facts:

- Self-harm is a way of expressing, and sometimes the only way of communicating pent-up, over-powering feelings.
- In many cases, self-harm can distract the person from suicide.

There are some official definitions of self-harm which reflect the view that this behaviour occurs during a state of distress and that the intention is not to die by suicide:

> '[Self-harm is] a state in which an individual is at high risk to injure but not kill themselves, and that produces tissue damage and tension relief.'
> (*Mosby's Medical, Nursing, and Allied Health Dictionary*, 1994)

'[Self-harm is] an expression of personal distress usually made in private, by an individual who hurts him or herself.'

(National Institute for
Clinical Excellence, 2004)

'[Self-harm is] deliberate harm to one's own body ... done to oneself, without the aid of another person.'

(Winchel and Stanley, 1991)

'[Self-harm is] an act with a non-fatal outcome, in which an individual deliberately initiates a non-habitual behaviour that, without intervention from others, will cause self-harm, or deliberately ingests a substance in excess of the prescribed or generally recognised therapeutic dosage, and which is aimed at realising changes which the subject desired via the actual or expected physical consequences.'

(Platt et al., 1992)

'The nature and meaning of self-harm ... vary greatly from person to person ... [it] may be different on each occasion and should not be presumed to be the same.'

(National Institute for
Clinical Excellence, 2004)

I have often been asked whether self-harm is a new phenomenon or whether incidences of it are increasing. Self-harm has been around for quite a while, but maybe we are just now becoming more aware of the behaviours; maybe it is only now that we are strong enough to confront this behaviour so that we can understand and support the children who handle strong emotions in this way.

What About the Pain?

How many times have you had a paper cut or burned yourself with boiling water? It hurts, doesn't it? So it's hard to understand how people who deliberately self-harm can cope with the pain of it. People who self-harm separate their minds from their bodies; while they are hurting themselves they are caught up with the result of the wound – whether there is blood or not – rather than the pain. Granted, they do have a higher pain threshold than most people, but their dissociation or dream-like trance makes it seem as if their skin has no nerve endings.

Of course, these people eventually feel the often excruciating pain of their wounds, coupled with guilt and shame. For some, it is a reminder that they have punished themselves; for others, it reminds them that their physical pain is far easier to deal with than their emotional pain.

The Turmoil of Discovery

As I said at the beginning of this chapter, discovery usually happens by accident when a parent or family member walks in on the child as they are self-harming. The myriad of feelings can leave you in turmoil. Those feelings can range from anger, shame or disgust to pity, compassion or disbelief. One of the most enduring feelings for most parents is that of blame; parents will attempt to analyse their own parenting skills in order to discover the reason why the child began to self-harm in the first place.

For many, the initial feelings of sadness or pity can turn to anger. Some parents will think this is attention seeking or that their children are just copying their friends in school. However, even if either of these reasons is true, it does not escape the fact that your child is in distress and incapable of communicating that distress in any other way. Blame and anger will see-saw between you and your child. Part of you will think that you gave this child everything – what more do they want? – and the other part of you will look for something that could have happened in the past that caused your child to behave in this way. The guilt that parents have in abundance anyway will increase tenfold.

This new knowledge about your child's behaviour will have a serious effect on the way you communicate with them in the future. You will fret and worry about every word, instruction or action that you direct at them. You will be fearful that you might just send them over the top. You may very well resent the child because you have enough in your life to cope with and wonder how you will find the time and energy to deal with this new problem.

These feelings are common, but the danger is that you will be overwhelmed by them and that the accusations you level – particularly at yourself – will prohibit you from dealing with the problem and helping your child. Try to remember that all these feelings are not only normal but will pass – but only if you allow yourself to understand fully the functions of and reasons for self-harm and why your child behaves in this way. It is also an opportunity to look at the way you communicate with your child and the possibility of changing it if it is necessary so that it will allow you and your child to learn and heal.

How to Identify a Self-Harming Child: What are the Warning Signs?

Young children (seven–twelve years of age) will show different signs to older children (thirteen–eighteen years). It is much harder to detect self-harm, or at least the early stages of self-harm, in young children because they look very much like normal 'war wounds' that can occur during play. Younger children may have scratches, scrapes or scabs that do not seem to be healing, or red marks from constant rubbing of the same area. Hair pulling – trichotillomania –that results in bald patches has often been mistaken for alopecia, leaving parents believing that their child is perhaps suffering from an iron deficiency. Trichotillomania is a compulsive disorder in which a person plucks out their hair strand by strand, but for a lot of children, pulling out their hair can occur as a distraction, in particular when the child is anxious. Head banging is another form of self-harm in the very young child.

The older child uses harsher methods of self-harm. The most important fact about this behaviour is that it is progressive – emotionally and physically. The young teenager will, like the young child, start off by possibly scratching with a fingernail, pin or the point of a compass, but they will progress quite quickly to cutting themselves with broken glass, broken crockery and, ultimately, blades and knives. While obviously the telltale signs are mild scars on the arms and legs, remember that most children keep this behaviour so hidden and so private that they have become masters of secrecy, so it is rare that you will just happen to see their wounds. Look out for the following:

- If you have spotted wounds and have questioned them, take note if your child gives weak excuses such as, 'I fell into a bush', 'I didn't see the barbed wire', or, 'the cat/dog scratched me'. If these reasons for the injuries are repeated, then there is a good chance that your child is self-harming.
- Clothing is another indicator. The self-harmer will change the way they dress in order to hide their injuries. Long sleeves and trousers are worn even in hot weather to cover up. Refusal to go swimming or to participate in an activity that would reveal flesh is a strong indication that self-harm is taking place.
- One very strong indicator that self-harming is taking place, which indeed cannot be explained away as anything other than that, is if you find a store of instruments that can cut or scratch. The obvious ones are, of course, razor blades, knives and pieces of glass, but there are some that are not so obvious, such as paper clips, large needles (like a darning needle), cigarette lighters or matches (not for smoking cigarettes but for burning themselves).

Sometimes you may see very little of the above behaviours, either because your child is extra careful – for example, a lot of young people will cut their stomach so that their scars will be well hidden – or because they are particularly good at hiding their objects. But there are also behavioural changes that take place that can otherwise be mistaken for 'normal' teenage behaviour:

- The child's secrecy should alert you that something is wrong. While most young people during their teens begin to withdraw from their parents, spending time in their bedrooms, etc., there is an emotional withdrawal also where your child may seem distracted or preoccupied. Your child may disappear more than usual to their room or some other private place so that they can self-harm.
- Self-enforced isolation: the young person will spend more and more time alone. They may stop going out with their friends and refuse to participate in any family initiative.
- They may seem highly sensitive, easily hurt, or you may notice that they will distance themselves if there is any conflict between other members of the family.
- If a parent is annoyed or angry with the child, they may not respond; in fact, they might appear completely passive, giving the impression that they are not listening or not present.
- They may make disparaging remarks about themselves: they may say they are ugly, stupid, that everybody hates them or that they are too fat or too skinny.
- If they used to be outgoing, gregarious and talkative, now they may be quiet and only engage when forced to, their answers usually being monosyllabic.

- Anti-social behaviours may suddenly develop, such as alcohol or drug abuse, stealing, lying and being defiant by staying out late instead of coming home at the normal time.
- If a young person has developed self-harming behaviours, eating disorders can also develop in conjunction with them. At Pieta House, we have also discovered that while many young people will say that they haven't self-harmed for a long time, they have in fact developed an eating disorder, thus substituting one harmful behaviour for another. Anorexia and bulimia are serious disorders that can become life threatening.

For many parents, the first time they become aware that their child is self-harming is when informed by the school counsellor. This is probably the most difficult way to discover that your child self-harms. All of a sudden, a seemingly 'normal' child that comes from a 'normal' home is exposed as a child who self-harms that comes from, what? Dysfunctional parents? Abusive parents? A crazy family? You may now understand why your child has kept this behaviour so hidden – because this exposure is surely going to make people judge you.

Self-Harm Manifested as an Eating Disorder
To explore in brief the connection between disordered eating and self-harming behaviour, many young people who attend Pieta House presenting with self-harm tend also to have issues with food. For those whose issues have developed into serious eating disorders, we see that anorexia or bulimia alternate with self-harm rituals. In other words, when a young person 'stops'

self-harming, parents/therapists may miss out on the fact that they have replaced self-harming with calorie counting, purging and food restriction.

There are many outside factors that can cause a child to develop anorexia or bulimia. Probably the most causative factor in children with eating disorders is the importance of body image. The combination of media pressure and peer pressure is partially responsible for the wave of eating disorders that is affecting children as young as eight and nine years of age, but in particular affecting those (mostly girls) between the ages of thirteen and sixteen. Magazines and TV shows offer a deluge of information on how to lose weight and look fabulous. If we adults find it hard to resist these alluring messages, then how will young people resist them? I believe our image- and body-focused culture has been one of the main causes of an increase in eating disorders. This phenomenon is more acceptable than self-harm; indeed, people feel sympathy for young people who purge or stop eating.

In Pieta House we have often heard teenagers who are so caught up with what a body should look like state that they wish they could 'cut away the love handles' or 'slice off a couple of inches' from their thighs. The young person's mind is in a stormy, never-ending battle with their body; the child who self-harms, whether it is by self-mutilation, promiscuity, taking drugs or alcohol, starving, bingeing or vomiting, may be trying to punish their body for not being perfect.

Children will often begin by experimenting with diets and then more than likely move on to skipping meals. If any weight loss occurs it may spur them on to further decrease food intake. They may then begin more sinister weight-loss behaviours, such as purging or using laxatives. This may be in addition to over-exercise and, thus, it may result in an obsession with calorie control and using the weighing scales on an hourly basis. Some eating behaviours may seem innocent enough at first – playing with food, eating only the salad or potatoes – but alarm bells should ring when young people start saying that they had something to eat at lunch time or at their friend's house, so they're not hungry now.

These behaviours, of course, fulfil the same need as those of self-harming – they are a distraction from emotional distress. Controlled eating can also serve to offset the feeling of having no control. That initial, short-lived rush of calm a young person feels after cutting or hurting themselves is similar to the satisfaction an anorexic feels when they deprive themselves of food, admiring their own sense of control. Their eating disorder is fulfilling a need that is not being met in other areas of their life.

Although anorexia and bulimia are in the same box as other self-harming behaviours, an eating disorder carries more dangers. Obviously the body's reaction to food restriction is life threatening, and if the child survives this, they may have caused untold damage that could last a lifetime.

Please do not become overly paranoid about your child's eating – they could of course be going through short-term finicky eating patterns that will never develop into an illness. However, here are some triggers and indicators that a young person has developed an eating disorder:

- Low self-esteem, though common in most young people, can become overwhelming, with feelings of inadequacy and low self-worth.
- When a person defines themselves in terms of how they look physically or how people view them.
- Eating disorders can, of course, commence when the young person in reality is overweight.
- As with self-harm, someone who develops an eating disorder finds it difficult to express, communicate or verbalise their emotions.
- When things are chaotic or out of control in their lives, developing an eating disorder puts control firmly back in the young person's hands.

Although eating disorders can become a replacement or a temporary alternative to other self-harming behaviours, we do not specifically treat this disorder in Pieta House, nor would I add it to the usual list of self-harming practices. This is because of the dangerous and secretive nature of anorexia and bulimia. People with this illness need long-term, specialised treatment. I believe that nutritional supervision and psychotherapy are the only ways to help a young person cope with life traumas manifesting themselves as eating disorders and the young person should be helped in a way that does not allow substitution to take place. This type of treatment may be over a long period and could possibly involve the whole family.

On discovering that your child engages in self-harming behaviour, besides going into shock, your next desire might be to confront, comfort, interrogate, soothe, shout or croon – perhaps all of these at the one time! But before you do anything, before you can even consider following any route, you need to arm yourself with knowledge. You need to find out why your child self-harms: what is the function and purpose behind this behaviour, what happened that made your child self-harm in the first place, what is going on that triggered this behaviour? Once you are fully informed, you will be able to help and heal your child.

Chapter Three
Why Do Children Self-Harm?

Children self-harm because they are unable to communicate their distress, and so their body becomes a canvas that expresses their overwhelming feelings. The reason self-harm is such a hidden behaviour is because once other people find out about it, they usually react with shock, disgust and anger – the very feelings the child already has about themselves. Self-harm indicates great distress; it is a sign that the child is trying to cope and carry on with their life despite their anxiety and emotional pain. The wounds are usually superficial and rarely life threatening, but they reflect not only the child's inner turmoil, but also their desire to 'kill' their feelings.

Although self-harm may seem damaging and destructive, the reasons behind hurting oneself are varied and complex, and differ from child to child. This chapter will answer the following questions:

- Who, statistically, is more likely to self-harm? A look at the 'typical' self-harmer.
- What life events/experiences have occurred that would cause a child to self-harm?

- Why self-harm? What are the functions behind this behaviour?

Who?

It is difficult to provide statistics that will portray the true figures of children who self-harm. This is mainly because of the private, secretive nature of the behaviour, though it is due partly to the fact that previous studies categorised self-harm as failed suicide attempts. However, studies do show certain common denominators:

- One in ten young people will self-harm at some point in their teenage years (Samaritans and Centre for Suicide Research, University of Oxford, 2002).
- Female children are four times more likely to self-harm than male children.

In Pieta House, we have discovered that the possible reasons for this second statistic is that boys are more likely to turn their emotions outwards, directing their aggression at others – picking fights, blaming sporting activities as the cause of the injury, etc. Girls direct their feelings inwards. Boys are less likely than girls to seek help and, later on, boys tend to turn to alcohol and drugs that will 'deaden' their emotions. Once again, our experience at Pieta House has made us realise that although boys handle their emotional distress differently to girls, both sexes are reacting to the same underlying problems and difficulties.

- Although self-harm can start at any age, the average age is around twelve years. Self-harm tends to peak around fifteen or sixteen years. The length of time a person self-harms can vary: it could be a once-off episode or a behaviour that lasts twenty or more years (cited in Mental Health Foundation, 2005).
- Children who self-harm have more problems and have had more critical life events than other children (Samaritans and Centre for Suicide Research, 2002).
- Cutting seems to be the preferred choice: 90 per cent of young people use this method (Board of Clinical Social Workers, 1997).
- A more recent study in Scotland found that in the age group of twenty–twenty-four years, more males were treated for self-cutting than females (cited in Mental Health Foundation, 2005). There is need for caution with this figure, however, because in Pieta House we have seen males who impulsively self-cut out of frustration or anger, usually on a once-off basis. People who consistently self-harm by cutting avoid public knowledge.
- One final alarming statistic: a national interview survey was carried out in England and it found that between 5 and 7 per cent of eleven–fifteen year olds self-harm (Meltzer et al., 2002). A 2005 study took place in Cork for which a registry of self-harm incidents was recorded. From 1 July to 31 December 2005, there were 2,967 presentations of self-harm to three Cork hospitals. Of this group, 21 per cent were under the age of fourteen.

This figure, of course, does not include the many thousands of young people who self-harm and who tend to their own wounds or sleep off the overdose.

What?

What life events cause a child to self-harm? What has happened that is so terrible that forces someone to inflict pain and damage on their bodies? Studies have shown that there are certain life events that children have experienced that cause the onset of self-harm.

PARENTAL ILLNESS OR ADDICTION

We parents are often unaware of how much knowledge children have of our lives. We exclude our children from knowing any of our problems, often out of protectiveness. We feel that they are unable to deal with the truth, so we tell them nothing. However, our children are much more perceptive than we give them credit for. They have an in-built curiosity. They need to discover and explore our world to learn how to survive. It may seem kind if we exclude them from difficulties that we have to face, but how will they learn when eventually they are faced with their own problems? They must learn from us.

If a parent is ill, a child's sense of security is at risk. They do not know what is happening – whether the parent will die or survive. They need to be advised, informed and included, though obviously in a sensitive way; otherwise their lives become fearful and uncertain.

If a parent has an addiction, whether it is to alcohol or drugs, the chaotic life that addiction brings to the home will also bring chaos and with it a tremendous fear to your child. The child has no control over these events, yet they are its most immediate victims.

If the child cannot verbalise their fear, this enormous emotion has to come out some way. For some children, self-harming is like opening a release valve; for others it allows them to focus and be distracted by physical pain rather than emotional pain.

Sexual abuse

Sexual abuse is the most understandable explanation for a child to turn to self-harm. For many young people, the abuse that was directed at them is, in turn, directed at their own body, which has become the physical embodiment of the evil inflicted upon them. They cannot punish the perpetrator, and so they punish the 'cause' of the shame. The self-harm injuries inflicted by young people who have been sexually abused are usually the most damaging, particularly around the sexual organs.

Emotional neglect/abuse

One theme that recurs in Pieta House is that children feel a profound sense of something missing in their relationship with their parent. If there is a lack of bonding or attachment, the child feels that the parent is almost indifferent to their problems, their feelings, their life.

In many cases, the parent themselves have suffered the same emotional neglect. The lack of nurture as a child means that they cannot provide it for their child. They experienced a lack of interest or bland indifference, and it has now been passed on. There are also cases where a parent is extremely harsh and critical of a child, using emotional blackmail as a weapon and communicating with directives and negative comments.

In both these cases, the child is growing up in an atmosphere that is a breeding ground for poor self-esteem. In this situation, the child self-harms as a form of punishment: they see themselves as 'unlovable' – it is their fault that the parent cannot show them love or affection.

PHYSICAL NEGLECT/ABUSE

Many of us take for granted that people will care for and protect their child. However, there are people who have experienced neglect and physical abuse as children and, therefore, see this as the norm. While some children who self-harm come from normal, stable homes, there are many who come from chaotic, unstable environments. Sometimes neglect can come about as a result of parental depression, where the caregiver is unable to look after the basic physical and emotional needs of a child. If there is a chaotic family event, such as a divorce or a death, the child can be overlooked or forgotten. Deliberate physical neglect or abuse, or the absence of the caregiver – emotionally and physically – can cause a child to feel incessantly and profoundly insecure, in danger and utterly unloved. Here children hurt themselves so that they can be distracted by physical pain and sometimes so that they can play the role of 'loving minder' to themselves, cleaning and patching up their own wounds.

EXTREME LACK OF COMMUNICATION

Talking is one of our most vital tools and is the most precious gift we can pass on to our children. Babies learn to communicate by imitating the parent. The parent will nod and coo and speak to the newborn; more importantly, the parent will act as if the child is 'talking back'. This is just the beginning of teaching the child to communicate. For example, 'Oh that's a big, big yawn! Is my baby very tired?' Communication further develops when the parent starts naming and acknowledging emotional states; for example, 'Did the big bear on the television frighten you?' Not only is the parent naming the emotion, but also acknowledging that it is acceptable, normal and expected of people to express emotions.

A young child needs to develop a relationship with a caregiver in order to develop social and emotional skills that will allow them to interact with the world (Bowlby, 1951). When communication and attachment are absent in the early stages, when an infant is developing in a world that is somewhat silent, the child will use the only tool they possess at this stage to communicate to their guardian: their cry. Although the parent will more than likely respond to the crying, a very clear message is being sent here: if the child expresses distress, the parent will react. At least the child's basic needs are being met, even without dialogue. But what happens when the child gets older and either crying is not acceptable anymore or the parent's response has been replaced by indifference? When there is no significant communication between a parent and the older child, when there is no talking about feelings or acknowledging a child's emotional state, the child has to convey their emotions in some way and, sadly, that way is usually through their body.

We are aware that thousands of children go through life events that have just been described, as well as other events such as bullying, witnessing family violence, excessively high expectations from parents, yet they manage to cope with these events and do not self-harm. So why do some children self-harm and others do not?

The reason is that when a child experiences an event that causes them to feel intense and distressing emotions, this feeling, coupled with the absence of the right kind of communication and support, creates an invalidating environment. Many of us will say that there were events in our childhood that were distressing and difficult but did not lead us to resort to self-harm. More often than not, however, we survived them and came out the other end unscathed because we had people in our lives who validated our feelings, empathised with us, listened to us and confirmed that what we were going through was tough.

Why?

One of the most frequent questions asked by parents and others is, why self-harm? Why choose that as an answer to turmoil? But then you could also ask why people drink too much, drive too fast, comfort eat? Self-harm is just another way of coping with life's difficulties. The purpose of self-harm can be divided into two main categories:

1. To communicate
2. To calm or subdue strong emotions.

1. To communicate

Earlier I said that the body of the person who self-harms is like a blank canvas. Each scar, mark or wound tells its own story. One young girl who attended us at Pieta revealed the cuts on her arms, criss-cross in design, and I remember thinking that they were 'in bits'. It was the first time that I made the connection: her arms were communicating what she was feeling inside – she was 'in bits'.

Young people will use their bodies to express their moods, their needs. They are not just communicating to other people, they are also communicating to themselves. The wounds can communicate a need to punish themselves for whatever reason, a need for comfort and help, or a terrible act of anger that cannot for whatever reason be taken out on the person who deserves the anger, so therefore the child takes it out on themselves.

Wounds on the outside of the body can translate the unbearable pain as something tangible that can now be fixed, even if only temporarily.

2. To calm or subdue

Many young people who self-harm say that when they harm themselves, in particular by cutting, they feel calm, a momentary respite from their pain. People coming to Pieta House often say that it is much easier to cope and deal with physical pain than to deal with emotional pain. Their harming acts as a distraction from the inner turmoil.

For some, cutting is a way of not just releasing pent-up emotions, but also acts as a cleansing mechanism that releases imagined toxins from their bodies. Many young people have taken tablets, such as paracetamol, not in an attempt at suicide, but in the hope that it will act as an analgesic for their emotional pain.

To understand why a child self-harms, we need to firstly look at the feelings that precipitate self-harm. They are normal, natural feelings that everyone at some stage in their life may feel, but these feelings are closely linked with an event that took place right before the child began to self-harm. Remember that your child, for whatever reason, is unable to communicate or verbalise whatever emotions they are feeling. They have developed a coping mechanism that allows them to express the built-up feelings that have been subdued over time. The tragedy is that the child will use this method of expression for every emotion, some of which we will now look at.

EMOTIONAL PAIN
Sadness, grief, despair, hopelessness: these feelings could be a result of many life events, such as the death or illness of a parent, parental separation or parental addiction, problems at school or with peers.

Self-harm in the form of an eating disorder, as an example, allows control back into the child's life. The anger that may be felt towards the parent, for example, can now be expressed indirectly: refusing to eat food brings about feelings of despair, fear and helplessness in a parent – the same feelings the child may be experiencing.

The inability to use the language of emotion means that a child cannot find the words to express what is going on inside them. Anger is the main emotion that children who self-harm say they feel – but they may use this same word for every negative emotion. They find it difficult to distinguish one distressing emotion from another.

The connection between the mind and the body may either have never existed or they have lost that ability to link what they feel with what they say. The child has learned that words do not work. The only language they can use now is the language of action.

Of course, there are many parents who are loving and sensitive to their child, who would talk through problems with their child, if only their child would tell them what the problem is. Many young children who self-harm may not have the vocabulary to express their pain. A wound can evoke much sympathy, compassion and nurturing, whereas words can be so inadequate, so limited in trying to explain pain. Communicating through self-harm tells a story that has gone unheard before, a picture that has not been viewed, a secret that is dying to be exposed.

ANXIETY

Feelings of fear, tension and panic are very often so overwhelming that even people who do not self-harm end up having panic attacks, developing disorders such as social phobias, obsessive compulsive disorder and other anxiety-driven behaviours.

Most of these anxiety disorders can be 'smothered' with medication such as Xanax or Valium, which dampen and subdue the fears. Of course, these forms of medication can be addictive and if not used properly can cause further problems. These anxieties have been there since birth for many people. We forget that children can have a seriously anxious nature and because they are too young to be 'medicated' their distress is ignored. They then resort to self-harm.

As adults, we all know, even if we haven't experienced it, what a panic attack is: when anxiousness and agitation escalate into bodily sensations. People suffering from a panic attack will have a pounding heart and sweaty hands; their throat will restrict and they will find it so difficult to breathe that they are afraid they are going to die that very minute. Imagine feeling like that at eleven years of age.

For so many children, the only treatment is cutting. The sense of relief is enormous – they begin to feel calm and their anxiety is relieved. The unrelenting thoughts begin to subside and the body state becomes normalised. Research has shown that in these situations, the brain releases chemicals called endorphins that act as an analgesic, the function of which is to help the body relax.

NEEDINESS

Young people who hurt themselves out of neediness do so because they feel unsupported and unheard. Nobody is validating their hurt; nobody is giving them the opportunity to voice their pain. A young child knows, either instinctively or from watching other people, that when they are hurt – emotionally or physically – the adult's natural reaction is to mind the child, soothe their wounds, rub the injury so that the child is 'all better'. When this physical and emotional attention is missing, the child can learn to substitute the absence of nurture with self-harm.

Unfortunately, the behaviour they choose is met with disdain and disgust. In Pieta House, we have seen that sometimes self-harm injuries get worse – the child may engage in more life-threatening behaviours, such as overdosing or not eating, just to have someone rescue them. When still ignored, the child's self-harm can take on a parenting role, as mentioned before – the child 'mothers' themselves. By hurting themselves, the child then has an opportunity to 'make it all better'.

ATTENTION NEEDING

Although most self-harming behaviours are hidden, there are some children who willingly reveal their wounds and deliberately expose their scars. Unfortunately, this has always been interpreted as 'attention seeking', but, as I mentioned earlier, attention seeking is in effect attention needing. These children are speaking loudly and clearly with their bodies: they are saying 'please mind me'. The neediness comes from neglect: the need to be cared for, loved, the need for some attention. The need has now gone to the ultimate extreme and the child has damaged their body in order to get someone to tend to them.

SELF-HATRED

Self-harm, cutting in particular, is sometimes viewed by the young person as a way of cleansing: letting the badness out or getting rid of the evil inside them. This self-hatred is usually a result of extreme trauma involving abuse. The child can also see self-harm as a way to punish themselves for being so evil or bad.

A child might also self-harm as a way to 're-enact' and expunge a past experience, usually sexual abuse. Many young girls who have been abused have cut their breasts or vaginas because they see them as 'dirty'. The wound is a corrective measure for a profoundly painful experience. The internal pain has now been placed on the outside.

UNREALITY

Many young people who self-harm often talk about how they feel disconnected from their bodies; they sometimes express feelings of numbness or deadness. When a person has a history of trauma, in particular if they were abused as a young child, they usually develop a coping strategy of dissociation. This allows the child to distance themselves from their body and their environment. By numbing themselves, on a physical and emotional level, they can deliberately make themselves unaware of what's happening to them and around them. In this situation, dissociation is a safety switch that can be turned on and off as needed.

However, dissociation can return even when there is no external threat and this can be a frightening experience for the person. It can be profoundly uncomfortable, to the point where the person feels they are losing their mind. Children in this situation self-harm in order to jolt themselves back into reality: the pain gets them back in touch with themselves. For people who feel dehumanised, cutting, which will inevitably cause bleeding, sometimes reassures the person that they are indeed human, that they are alive.

ANGER

Anger is one of the most common emotions young people find difficult to express. We, as parents or teachers, constantly tell our children that they are not allowed to show anger or indeed be angry. Yet most of us have acted out our anger by shouting, slamming doors or by being aggressive, and most of us have learned how to contain that anger. However, for some children, self-harm is a better option. They may have grown up in families where anger and violence were closely linked, so they are unable to separate the feeling and the behaviour and believe that one inevitably follows the other. To them, it is easier and far better to hurt themselves than to lash out at someone else.

Anger for many young people feels out of control; self-harming gives back that feeling of power – over their own body – when everything around them seems to be chaotic and confused. Maybe for the first time, or the only time, the young person feels a sense of autonomy; they feel in charge of something.

To Summarise
Certain circumstances in family situations can be a causative factor in the commencement of a child's self-harming behaviour. In brief, these are as follows:

- When there is a traumatic loss, such as parental death, or when there is a serious illness within the family. Perhaps a parent or a sibling is ill; sometimes the child themselves is ill, resulting in hospitalisation and enforced separation from the child's parents.
- Where there is the breakdown or the non-uptake of family roles, where children have to take on adult responsibilities or where they are forced to 'befriend' a parent, in so doing becoming a parent to their parent.

- Where there is neglect and/or abuse: physical, sexual and emotional.
- Parental fragility, where a parent, because of their own upbringing, is unable to respond appropriately to the emotional needs of their child.
- Depression, where a parent, due to their own difficulties, is unable to connect or cope with the physical and emotional needs of their child.

There is no such thing as a typical person who self-harms. Psychologists are still perplexed by the notion that although two children may experience the same trauma, both children will respond differently: one may turn to self-harming, the other may not. While we realise that the child who does not self-harm will, more than likely, have a supportive relationship with someone, we must also consider that there are far more complex factors involved. We need to consider the child's capacity to cope and deal with difficult and traumatic situations; their ability to adapt to different circumstances. We also need to consider society's role and how its acceptance of certain behaviours from celebrities can manipulate a child into believing that self-harm is not only acceptable, but almost a badge of belonging. The next chapter will deal with this form of pressure, among others.

Chapter Four
The Child Who Self-Harms and Society's Influence

While this book has concerned itself so far mainly with parental and familial influences that may cause a child to start self-harming, we are also aware that the society and culture we live in today can foster and in some ways encourage self-harming behaviours. There are three main areas of external influence: media pressure, peer/cult pressure, and cultural changes.

Media Pressure
The media can influence our beliefs, our core values, our opinions, and many of us base what we perceive as 'normal' on what we see on television, hear on radio or read in magaines. The media plays an important role in the way our children view themselves and their world. Television and the internet both have a great influence on children's views. We are constantly bombarded with 'perfect' images – the perfect face, the perfect body – and we are told how to attain this perfection. Our girls, in particular, are growing up in a society that sends out intense and conflicting messages about their bodies. Newspaper articles, magazines and television programmes emphasise the importance of having the correct

shape in order to be attractive, popular and happy. This enormous pressure to judge and be judged, to strive for and attain the perfect body is something that most teenagers struggle with but eventually come to terms with. For the vulnerable young person, however, this is just one more thing that makes them feel bad about themselves.

Over the years there have been a number of celebrities who have admitted using self-harm to cope with their traumatic situations. Princess Diana, in her famous interview with Martin Bashir, said how engaging in self-harming behaviour helped her cope with her husband's infidelities. Johnny Depp and the comedienne Roseanne Barr have also spoken about their self-harming behaviour. More recently, the singer Amy Winehouse has publicly displayed signs of self-harming, speaking about it as a way of coping. The problem with this type of very public demonstration is that young people now become intrigued, wondering if it 'works'. Engaging in similar behaviour also gives them a link to public and popular figures.

Growth of this behaviour has exploded over the years and we at Pieta House have noticed that self-harm is almost suggestive. For the majority of people who self-harm, it comes naturally to them; however, there are those who begin self-harming because they heard somewhere that it 'works', that it is a really good stress buster, a coping tool for the twenty-first century! Media exposure of the behaviour, while necessary and helpful in highlighting the problem and in dragging it out from under the carpet, may also have caused a phenomenon called 'contagion' – in other words, giving our young people new ideas.

Our young people take their cues not only from the media and from celebrity behaviour, but also from their friends. Many of the children who come to Pieta House have a friend who self-harms or knows somebody who self-harms. For some, they knew about self-harm either from a sibling, from a magazine article, or from a parent who also self-harmed.

But let's remind ourselves that the typical, well-adjusted young person would not begin this type of behaviour had they the necessary coping tools to allow them to deal with whatever life throws at them. They may have tried to self-harm, out of curiosity, but discovered that it actually hurt and so would not continue with it. It is the vulnerable child who may grab a solution with both hands to see if it works, to see if it helps them deal not only with present difficulties but with the agonies of the past.

Peer and Cult Pressure

I often wonder if we underestimate the enormity of the change that children experience when they enter secondary school. They come from a primary school system where all that is required of them is a passive response. Things change dramatically when they start secondary school. They are thrust into an environment that is noisy and clamorous, a place where only the fittest survive! Immediately they are expected to adapt to new rules, new structures and new responsibilities. On top of all that they are suddenly surrounded by hundreds of people, most of whom they don't know. They have to get used to new subjects, new languages and teachers who usually have only forty minutes to pass on their knowledge. If that isn't enough, they have to deal with bodily changes and hormones that are starting to cause havoc. But I suppose the most important task of all for this child, one which we may not be aware of, is that of a development of their identity. This young person needs to know who they are, what they stand for and how others view them. This struggle often leads the teenager into rebellious and irritable episodes in an attempt to separate themselves from the confines of their parents' claustrophobic clutches. Their moods vacillate: one minute they seem very mature, the next they are hitting their younger brother because 'he hit me first'. This is all very normal stuff: very challenging, but also very much part of the normal processes of finding oneself.

For many young people, discovering their own identity, 'who they are', is difficult but manageable. They may go in and out of different phases, follow different 'looks', but eventually they settle down and find their own likes and dislikes, their own style, their own music.

For the vulnerable child, however, this searching can take an upsetting turn. Children who come from difficult backgrounds – who have been deprived of parental love and attention, who have witnessed injustice, violence or indifference – are poorly armed or prepared for this stage of their life. If they arrive at adolescence without having experienced the protection and safety of a normal childhood, then these new challenges represent hurdles that seem onerous and insurmountable. This is a time when so many changes are happening on so many fronts, where they will have to rely heavily on their own devices and on coping skills that have never been taught. Their immature or underdeveloped coping skills, their poor self-esteem and, in particular, their lack of adult support will make the next few years very difficult.

The child who does not believe in themselves, whose self-esteem is so low that they do not have the confidence to even attempt to form their own identity, may turn to people who also have low self-esteem. Some young people will adopt an identity and become a Goth or Emo. And while for most young people this will be a harmless phase, for other more vulnerable young people these identities will be a very negative way to channel their problems by self-harming. To the young and vulnerable, they provide an instant, off-the-shelf identity.

Self-harming is part of the 'conditions' of membership, though many young people who say they are Emos or Goths do not self-harm. If you look at the Facebook or Bebo pages of some Emos or Goths, you will see pictures of young people revealing their wounds to an audience of other young and vulnerable people. These socially lost children are acting out their hurt and using the cloak of a cult to be socially included and to allow them to feel like they belong. For any parent out there who has a child who belongs to one of these social groups, it may just be a harmless phase – a bit like the Mods and Rockers of the 1960s – but it might also be more serious.

Continuing on from the topic of social networking sites, today the most powerful form of media for young people is the internet. Children, young people and adults spend hours in front of a screen, which becomes their main social outlet and allows them to share themselves, be it through the divulging of personal information and opinions or the sharing of photographs. This means that our children are not just consumers of media but also creators. Many young people use these sites to make new friends or to get something off their chest. An attractive forum for young people, it can be a springboard for more unsavoury activities. The dangers that our young people are exposed to include sites that detail how to self-harm and even more sinister sites on how to die by suicide. Membership of these groups can validate a young person's self-harming behaviour and make it acceptable. Contagion is growing whereby young people are learning from each other how to self-harm, and with the wonders of technology they can even synchronise their activities so that they self-harm at the same time.

Cultural Changes

It would seem that our communities are slowly but surely changing into soulless places where the new religion is money and the new church is the sprawling shopping centre. Instant gratification is the norm: fast foods, faster access to the internet, faster ways of seeking pleasure. We are not allowed to feel anything that would be remotely negative – sad, depressed or worried; we must rid ourselves of the feeling immediately, so we take a tablet or reach for a drink.

The extended family seems to be collapsing; the support that used to come from grandparents, relatives and neighbours is lessening. Thus, people feel increasingly isolated, as though they have no one to whom they can turn in a time of crisis. Homes have become mini apartment blocks; gone are the days when the family would gather around the television together, not to mention gather together in prayer. Everyone eats, sleeps and practically lives in their own bedroom, which is fitted out with cable TV, PlayStations and music systems.

Although the unsupervised child might enjoy being able to watch whatever they like on TV, they are becoming more isolated. Both the child and the parent are missing opportunities for communication. These new arrangements can make it nearly impossible for parents to simply enquire as to how their child is feeling.

More and more parents work outside the home and while the added income for some has made life and leisure time more enjoyable, for most parents it is necessary for both to work in order to afford many of the basics. While most nannies, crèches and child-minders are professional, caring and loving towards our children, unfortunately it may mean that our children are being reared by strangers. The danger is that when there are several 'minders' there is no consistency, and attachment becomes fragile or non-existent.

As our children get older, we allow them to come home by themselves, once again unsupervised. They are rearing themselves. The parents more than likely feel guilty over the lack of parental supervision, so they give in to the child's every whim. As a working parent, I know the pitfalls and also the stress we go through to keep down a job and rear a family at the same time. I know that there are times we have to make decisions that do not always seem to be in the best interest of the child – such as having the children arrive home before us or leaving them with different minders when the regular minder is on holidays. We do our best and our best is usually good enough so that it causes little or no damage to our children. However, we must remain vigilant. As a society, we need to face up to our input as guardians and take responsibility for whatever mistakes we may have made with our children. We must make time for our children in this busy world. We must stop and listen, truly listen to what they are saying or trying to say. There is nobody who knows your child better than you. Children need boundaries, but as well as that they need to be heard, and they need to know that you are their biggest supporter. It is in such an environment that they will thrive.

Chapter Five
Disorders That Can Cause a Child to Self-Harm

There are three groups of people who attend Pieta House that could be viewed as coming from normal, nurturing backgrounds, but who self-harm. These groups are young people who may have been diagnosed with a Borderline Personality Disorder (BPD), as a Highly Sensitive Child (HSC) or someone who might have a diagnosis of Asperger's Syndrome.

Borderline Personality Disorder

This disorder is probably the most often connected to people who self-harm. For the sufferer there is a lack of emotional regulation and periods of emotional intensity, in particular when the young person is under stress. Young people with BPD seem to be their own worst enemy, to the point of almost inviting unloving responses and ultimately rejection. They can appear hostile and demanding, and family members, understandably, can find it increasingly difficult to form a loving bond with them.

BPD is a disorder that develops over years in line with the development of the child's personality. Personality disorders are usually diagnosed by late adolescence or early adulthood (early twenties), when the personality is generally considered to be fully developed. There are often occasions when a person is not diagnosed until well into adulthood, but this does not mean that the disorder has just manifested itself, only that it was not previously diagnosed.

This is a controversial topic. Many experts have argued that BPD should not be diagnosed in anyone younger than eighteen because their personality is not yet fully formed until then. However, in the most recent edition of the *Diagnostic and Statistical Manual of Mental Disorders*, there is a stipulation that allows for the diagnosis of BPD before the age of eighteen. There is also a condition that allows, in rare cases, children under the age of thirteen to be diagnosed.

The good news is that it is possible that the symptoms and level of dysfunction ebb and flow over time, and for many the level of instability and the intensity of BPD symptoms even off as a person enters mid to late adulthood. Please remember that a diagnosis of BPD, just like any other disorder, should be nothing more than a name that allows us to categorise the symptoms and the functioning levels a person may be operating on. We can then allow a correct diagnosis to provide answers to the people who suffer with this disorder and to those who care about them, which will help everyone – patient, family and clinicians – make sense of confusing and painful feelings and experiences.

For a diagnosis to be made, at least five of the following symptoms must be present:

REJECTION/ABANDONMENT SENSITIVITY
This is probably the most obvious of symptoms. The person has an exaggerated fear of being rejected

or abandoned, and because it causes such strong emotional reactions in people with BPD they will often attempt to reduce their terrible fears of being abandoned by 'checking in' on the person that they are in a relationship with (parent, friend, etc.). They do this through constant contact, such as texting, ringing, etc. While they may be reassuring themselves, they are, unfortunately, creating the very scenario they are in fear of – rejection and avoidance by other people. They can also react very strongly and dramatically to trivial rejections by others: for example, if someone needs to delay or cancel a plan or engagement, their fear becomes so intense that they can become enraged with the person, which, of course, further damages the relationship.

Mood Swings

Many people who suffer from BPD experience mood swings that are difficult to move on from. Anger in particular can be extreme and out of control. Sufferers can feel intense anger that is out of proportion to the situation at hand and they have great difficulty controlling this emotion. On many occasions, this can result in dramatic behaviours such as shouting, breaking things or even assaulting people. They also go through great states of anxiety and unhappiness.

Relationship Difficulties

As mentioned previously, the fear of abandonment can cause difficulty in relationships and many sufferers have great difficulty in participating in and maintaining relationships. The relationships that they do have can usually be very intense with lots of conflict. Their emotions towards a person can swing from adoration to intense hatred and they can often feel great disappointment that the person they are focused on is not reacting to their neediness in the manner they would like.

EMPTINESS

People with BPD often speak about experiencing profound feelings of emptiness. This can cause great distress because the person with BPD can often feel numb, as if they had no emotions. This coupled with a distorted sense of identity can create intense despair and sadness.

SELF-HARM

Remember that people with BPD suffer very intense, usually very negative emotions. Sometimes these emotions are so distressing that they look for a way to escape them. They can come up with many different ways of reducing this emotional pain, the obvious ones being alcohol or drugs. However, many young people who cannot access such means resort to self-harm. Young people often say it is far easier to deal with and focus on physical pain than terrible inner distress and turmoil. Another symptom of BPD is impulsiveness, which, of course, means that the person has a tendency to act quickly without thinking of the consequences, leading to self-harm becoming a common occurrence.

SUICIDE

The impulsiveness trait of someone with BPD can also result in more serious consequences. Unfortunately, suicidal ideation, behaviours and completed suicides are very common. Research has shown that around 70 per cent of people with BPD will make at least one suicide attempt in their lifetime; many will make multiple suicide attempts.

People with BPD are more likely to complete suicide than individuals with any other psychiatric disorder. Between 8 and 10 per cent of people with BPD will complete suicide; this rate is more than fifty times the rate of suicide in the general population (P.H. Soloff et al., 1994; D.L. Gardner and R.W. Cowdry, 1985).

It is important to remember that some of the symptoms described above are experienced by many people from time to time, particularly by young people. However, people with BPD will experience several of these symptoms daily, or almost daily, for years. Remember, too, that people with BPD will show these symptoms across many different environments, such as relationship instability within family situations and outside of the family environment. As opposed to people who do not have BPD, it can be perfectly normal to have conflict within the home of growing teenagers and yet have stable relationships at school.

Many parents of BPD sufferers ask what they have done wrong. My answer to them is that a child does not suffer with BPD because of poor parenting skills. So many young people with the disorder come from families that are stable and healthy, with environments that contain the normal levels of family stress. It has been suggested that people with BPD might be biologically hypersensitive to normal family stress levels. What appears a normal, mildly emotive situation can seem like a most distressing emotional scenario for the person with BPD.

The symptoms of BPD should be viewed at all times as most distressing for the young person and we must realise that their self-harming is a real attempt to communicate their inner distress. As mentioned previously, diagnosis can be controversial and people often wonder about the relevance of same. I believe that a diagnosis should only be given if it can be used to describe a person's way of dealing with life and relating to others.

The Highly Sensitive Child

Some of the symptoms of BPD share a remarkable similarity to those belonging to the Highly Sensitive Child (HSC). The main difference I believe, however, is that the HSC is extensively more in tune with their environment and the people in it than the young person who has BPD, who is more caught up in themselves and their own turmoil.

Over the last few years we have seen an increasing number of very young children at Pieta House. These children are usually highly intelligent but very anxious. They seem to process external information or stimuli more thoroughly than other children. On a physical and emotional level, they seem to detect, process and then understand situations more profoundly than children and adults who are less sensitive.

On a physical level, there are many things that cause them chronic irritation, such as labels on the back of jumpers, socks that feel too tight, even sand under their feet or the texture of newspaper. They would be extra sensitive to nuances: for example, they notice if a room has changed, and there are certain smells that they cannot bear. On an emotional level, they are highly sensitive to how people react to them. They can 'feel' things to the extreme, such as sadness, anger and joy. People would often accuse them of being histrionic, over-dramatic, even attention seeking. The reality is that they are experiencing their feelings in a more dramatic and intense way compared to others.

Anxiety plays a big part in their everyday life. Their intelligence allows them to analyse everything. If they heard that someone was knocked down by a car, they could become very anxious in case they or a family member are knocked down. Any sort of change can also cause enormous anxiety: starting secondary school, for example, can be such a traumatic event for them that they would worry and fret for months.

Self-harm in children who are highly sensitive seems to be a bit of a paradox. They feel everything so acutely that you would assume they wouldn't cut or hurt themselves because the pain would be more intense and extreme. However, their anxiety reaches such a peak that it may be accompanied by a complete lack of physical sensation. Cutting or harming jolts them back.

Listed below are some of the common characteristics and qualities of someone who is a Highly Sensitive Child.

• These children are usually highly intuitive. They always know when 'something is up'. It is as if they are on constant alert to other people's emotions or actions. They interpret people's body language, their expressions, even their tone of voice. This sensitivity can have a downside, because they can be affected by people's moods – in particular, those of their parents.

- Certain smells, even bright colours, can cause distress to these sensitive children. They may dislike being tickled, walking through crowded areas or hearing loud noises (they can become very easily startled). Many such children become easily irritated over things that most people wouldn't notice.
- They are usually creative, kind, thoughtful and more than likely co-operative. They will experience our world more deeply and with a greater appreciation of nature and animals. If, however, they have had a few bad experiences, such as someone teasing them in school or an adult being impatient and insensitive with them, they become withdrawn, anxious and usually depressed. Remember, these negative feelings are felt with great intensity to the point where a child could begin to self-harm. As well as being overwhelmed by external stimulants, they can also be overwhelmed by internal processes. Their reaction to their emotions can be distressing for their family with dramatic, angry outbursts or the most despairing sobs.

Having a child who is highly sensitive will bring you on a roller coaster of emotions. Try to remind yourself that they feel they are drowning in a sea of intense emotions and sensations. You must be their life buoy. You will need extra patience, empathy and compassion. You will need to work with this child in a more intense way than with your other children. Besides having buckets of empathy and understanding for your child, you will need to have a very firm structure and solid boundaries in place. You will need to encourage them to take risks and teach them how to become aware of the intensity of their emotions so that they will learn to contain them themselves, rather than rely on you to monitor and contain them.

Asperger's Syndrome

This is another disorder that can be missed for many years; sometimes it is not identified until the late teens. The young people who come to Pieta House with this condition are usually in great distress. Their distress is wholly understandable because they are now placed in a situation where they are forced to communicate. The main issue concerning people with Asperger's is exactly that: although they have language fluency, they find it incredibly difficult to communicate on a social level, to get the words that are in their head out of their mouth, as one client explained it. This disorder, which affects mostly males, can be described as a set of behaviours ranging from poor social skills to poor coordination. What is important to recognise is that young people with Asperger's have normal language development and intelligence; their social skills are, however, very limited and they interact poorly with others. Listed below are some of the most obvious symptoms of this disorder.

- An inability to notice or interpret the body language of others, including facial expressions.
- A tendency to remain with the same facial expression at all times, showing little or no emotion.
- A failure to be aware of, or possibly displaying insensitivity to, the feelings of others.

- When talking, a lack of awareness if someone is listening or even interested in what they have to say. Conversation can be sporadic, involving random topics.
- An inability to understand jokes or comments that have a double meaning. Everything said by another is taken literally.
- An unusual obsessions with objects, routines or interests – this is more typical during early teen life. The danger is that it further impedes and interferes with the building of social interactions and relationships.
- At an early stage, a higher vocabulary level than children their own age. However, they may be quite pedantic in their conversation.
- Sometimes, an inability to play creatively and a difficulty using their imagination. However, many children with Asperger's are particularly good with facts and figures.
- Sometimes, an unusual sensitivity to sensory stimuli (such as the feel of certain materials).

So what causes Asperger's Syndrome? There has been much controversy over this: is it genetic or environmental? The assumption that emotional deprivation is a causative factor of Asperger's is not only incorrect but dangerous. Asperger's belongs to the continuum of Autism, a spectrum of behaviours ranging from very mild Asperger's to the far end of Autism. It is a neurobiological disorder that is still being extensively researched.

There are many other psychological and psychiatric disorders where a person will self-harm and it is symptomatic of their illness. These are serious problems where talking therapy is of no help in their treatment. However, Borderline Personality Disorder, Highly Sensitive Children and young people with Asperger's Syndrome can be dealt with effectively because they can engage with talking therapy, and compassion and encouragement will allow this child to move forward and enjoy a life with meaningful relationships.

Chapter Six
Parenting Issues

To parent a child means so many things. It means to love and nurture, to look after the physical and emotional aspects of your child, to be their teacher, their protector, their advocate and their biggest fan. You may have been able to look after the physical needs of your child when they were growing up: you made sure that they were warm, well nourished and clothed, and that they attended all the curricular and extra-curricular activities. You made sure they had birthday presents and visits to Santa – you even dressed up as Santa yourself! You tried to make sure that they had, within reason, everything they could possibly need. But maybe you have not been able to develop a connection with your child. Below I will look at some issues that might prompt self-harm within the family home, but again to say that self-harm does not necessarily arise from any of the following scenarios; children who self-harm often come from loving and supportive homes.

LACK OF COMMUNICATION
One of the most important tasks we have as a parent is to teach our child how to communicate. As I mentioned

briefly earlier, the next time you see a mother or father with a new infant, watch how they interact with the baby. Chances are that the parent will talk to the baby as if they already understand language. And what is truly remarkable, after the parent speaks to the baby, they then pause as if to listen to the infant responding. The parent talks for the child, which is the start of a very important learning plan. As the child gets a little older, the parent then starts naming objects and also tries to read their mind. For example, 'Do you want your bottle?' or 'Are you looking for your blanket?' This is the wonderful commencement of communication.

This process goes a step further, a very important step. The parent now begins naming feelings and emotions: 'Oh you poor thing, that loud noise frightened you'; 'I know you are sad because it's raining and you can't go out into the garden'; or 'I know you are feeling cross with mommy for not buying you sweets, but you know we have sweets at home'. These prompts that we give our children help them to name, express and accept that feelings are sometimes uncomfortable, but by verbalising them and in turn listening, their feelings will be validated.

If the child has never been taught how to name or express emotions, they will take action instead; if their feelings are invalidated or ignored they will also take action, because action is the only way they know how to relieve or express these emotions. Perhaps when you were growing up your needs were not met and so you cannot meet the emotional needs of your child. Maybe you come from a family where love, attention and emotional support were not available; you may have grown up in a family where the roles were reversed and you had to be the parent and rear your siblings; or you could have been separated from your parents because of long-term hospitalisation or, as was the case years ago in Ireland, because you were sent to live with an aunt or a grandmother who lived alone. That feeling of abandonment, even though you were still 'with family', would likely occur.

RIGID/OVERLY STRICT PARENTING
People whose parents enforced strict and rigid rules can find it hard to communicate with and show emotion to their children. Their parents used communication to scold and criticise. This type of environment left little room for loving communication and it did not allow normal emotive expressions. Feelings of sadness, anger, fear and vulnerability were put aside and were not allowed to be expressed.

SEXUAL ABUSE
It is widely believed that people self-harm because they were sexually abused as children. Although there are cases where this is true, the majority of children who self-harm live in an environment where no sexual abuse exists, but where they suffer different parental failings or psychological trauma that remains with them in adult life. However, it is vital that such a possibility be investigated because many studies indicate that sexual abuse in childhood leads onto self-harm and suicide in later life.

DISSOCIATION
There are usually a number of factors that bring about self-harm in children and, as mentioned before, we

need to take into account the emotional frailty of the child. I mentioned the term 'dissociation' earlier: an unintentional disconnection between the person's mind and what is being experienced by their body. It is usually a result of a profoundly traumatic incident or a series of incidents that has happened to the child. I have worked with children who have witnessed murder and suicide, who have watched their parents die in a car accident or through illness. As adults, we find it difficult to cope with these traumatic situations, but imagine how a child might cope, with or without support.

We all possess this ability to separate our mind and body, for good or not-so-good reasons. At Pieta House, we have met some parents who are disconnected from their child and remain so even when the child reveals their terrible wounds and their frightening thoughts. This isn't because the parent doesn't love their child, but rather because they feel 'cut off' from the reality and the horror of the situation. This is either a self-taught behaviour (perhaps something tragic happened to them as a child) or it is a learned behaviour; in other words, that was how they were treated as children and history is repeating itself.

Seeking Help and Improving Parenting Skills

For those of you who have been locked into your own personal problems and pain, maybe this is an opportunity for you to seek help. If that is not possible for you or if you do not want to unearth past agonies, then maybe you would consider a parenting course. These courses are fantastic. They really help parents come up with useful strategies that not only encourage acceptable and realistic boundaries between you and your children, but also teach you how to communicate with your child in a loving and supportive way. Indeed, I believe we should all do a parenting course as soon as we begin to have children, if not before. Barnados (a national charity that supports children and their families) has information on parenting courses – www.barnados.ie.

Positive Communication

Whether the difficulties and the present fall-out are because of you or your partner's childhood, or if they are the result of problems that have arisen as your children have grown up – such as illness, alcohol or substance abuse, or bereavement – it is never too late to change patterns of behaviour and learn skills that will enable you to support and empower your child.

The main thing that you need to look at is how you communicate with your child. When our children are very young, we tend to teach them how to do different tasks and our role becomes very much a teaching one. As they get older, we sometimes need to realise that our tactics have to change. One very useful exercise that I give to parents is to track or record how they communicate with their child. I hand them a sheet of paper with the following columns printed on it:

DIRECTIVES	NEGATIVE COMMENTS	POSITIVE AFFIRMATIONS

This record sheet is very simple. Over the period of one day, every time you give your child a directive (for example, 'Go and tidy your room', 'Empty the dishwasher' or, 'Have you finished your homework?' etc.), place a tick in the 'Directives' column.

Every time you give your child a negative comment (for example, 'You're not going out in that!', 'Look at the state of you – your face is plastered with make-up/your hair looks ridiculous' or, 'You eat too much, no wonder you're overweight!'), place a tick in that column.

Obviously, the same goes for the last column. Every time you give your child a positive affirmation (for example, 'I am so proud of you', 'That was a really kind thing you did for your brother' or, 'You have such lovely skin/you are so handsome/pretty'), place a tick in that column.

As you have probably guessed, the first two columns – 'Directives' and 'Negative Comments' – will more than likely have far more ticks than the last column, 'Positive Affirmations'. I believe every parent should try this exercise. It took the wind out of me when I completed it; no wonder our children might suffer from poor self-esteem. But this exercise not only tracks how you communicate with your child, but also encourages you to start changing the negative into the positive. If your child is a teenager, the exercise may show you that there are many activities that we need to leave up to them to do.

Awareness of Your Reaction to Emotions
Another aspect of communication is to show an interest in your child's day, their friends and their activities.

This is a wonderful opportunity to get to know your child's inner child. Through dialogue, your child could reveal, possibly without naming them, the fears and joys that they experience daily.

You may find initially that your teenager just shrugs and appears uninterested. Don't give up; your child has learned not to express their feelings verbally but to 'act' on them. You will just have to encourage dialogue, and even though at the beginning it may be 'all picture and no sound', you must keep trying.

Another useful exercise that will again increase your awareness of your child's behaviour, and one that can give you a deep insight into how difficult, shameful and embarrassing harming oneself can be, is to think about yourself and your own feelings and how you deal with them. Take three main feelings: anger, sadness and anxiety. How do you handle these very strong emotions?

- Do you go 'ballistic' when you are angry? Do you slam your fist on the table, punch or kick the wall? Do you shout and roar at everyone, slam doors? Do you sulk for hours or even days without interacting or speaking to anyone?
- Do you become introspective and withdrawn when you are sad? Do you drink to make yourself feel better? Do you stop caring for yourself – not washing your hair or having a shower? Do you cut yourself off – sit around moping all day?
- Do you become irritable, distracted and agitated when you are anxious? Do you drink more and smoke when these feelings occur? Do you bite your nails to the quick, or chew on the inside of

your cheek or bottom lip? Does your anxiety affect everyone else in the house, making even your children anxious?

If these are some of the reactions or behaviours that you participate in when you are emotionally overwhelmed, then you as an adult must see how much more difficult it is for a child. If you can, try to share with your child the proper way in which to handle or cope with emotions. Let them know that many people have difficulties in expressing pent-up feelings and not everyone gets them right. Doing this will alleviate some of the guilt and shame your child feels; it will also let them know that you understand, you are not angry and that you just want to help.

Reactions of Others

I think it is very important that you are mindful of the reactions of others if or when they hear about the behaviours of your child. Some reactions experienced by young people and related to us in Pieta House have included: condemnation for their wounds; being treated as if they were disturbed or 'crazy'; being greeted with shock and fear, even by those in the professional therapeutic realm; and in the medical realm itself, being treated as if the self-harming were purely a physical injury, rather than an emotional, psychological issue.

Think back to how you reacted when you discovered that they were harming themselves. Those who have never come across self-harm before will probably respond the way you did. If there is any negative reaction from people in the health service, remember that their primary role is to save lives, and when wounds are self-inflicted they may become disapproving or dismissive in their response. Try to understand the enormous pressure and stress they are under to protect life and that they are operating from a medical model, which means that if you are sick you are treated with medicine. Self-harm carries a lot of personal theories and diverse attitudes; as parents, you should be prepared to come across a lot of misunderstandings and opinions from people across the board. This is why it is essential that the people who matter to your child most will act in a calm, supportive way that does not add to the shame or disgust your child already feels.

Chapter Seven
What Can Parents Do?

When you begin any efforts to help your child end their self-damaging behaviour, more than likely they will be sceptical, dubious and downright disbelieving that they can stop self-harming and live normally. They will feel that they are giving up their best friend; that whatever they gain in giving up the practice, they will lose much more – the comfort, the calmness, the secret that they have been holding onto tightly.

Following on from the last chapter, think again about the way you communicate an emotion – let's take anger. Many people will shout and give out when they are angry; they may slam doors or stomp up the stairs; they may swear and curse; or they may be physically aggressive, banging their hands down on tables or hitting out at someone. This behaviour causes harm and hurt to other people.

If you asked these people to stop behaving this way, they would find it very difficult. Years of behaving like this have given them the desired result, whether that result is making that person feel better or manipulating situations to suit their own ends. It is the same with someone who self-harms. Their harming has served a purpose: it is an act of self-help and it fulfils many functions for them: as an emotion regulator, for example. The person who self-harms would equally, if not more so, find it difficult to stop this behaviour. Their experience has been that the feelings of comfort counteract the harm it is doing.

So both of these ways of dealing with anger are ineffective, but neither can be changed unless two things happen: first, the person must want to stop and change; second, they must replace that negative behaviour with a positive one.

Now What?

Now that you know your child self-harms you are faced with a dilemma. How do you confront the child? If you have been informed by a school counsellor or principal, the approach is much easier for you. The school has flagged your child's harming behaviours so you have an opportunity to deal with it and discuss it. If your child disclosed to the school counsellor, you are then in a better position of providing help because your child clearly wants help if he or she has asked for it already. If, however, the school found out because one of the other students informed the school counsellor, the situation may be a bit more difficult. You may find yourself facing great resistance to seeking a resolution to the problem. Regardless, the stage has been set and you need to plan the next strategy most carefully.

If you discovered by accident that your child self-harms – you walked in on them cutting themselves or you discovered bloodied tissues or blades – then unless you have superhuman control, you will more than likely immediately express your feelings of shock and disbelief. You will need, however, to wait until you are calmer and more informed to be in a position to address the problem. Please get it into your head that your child is not behaving in this way to 'get at' you. They are not 'weird', 'freaky' or 'strange'; they are just trying to cope. You must act swiftly though; ignoring it or thinking it is just a phase will not make it go away. Worse still, your child might now be aware that you know and your inaction might give them the message that you don't care.

Don't be afraid to be direct. Whatever way you found out, you need to say something like, 'Your teacher told me that you have been hurting yourself. I am so concerned for you and I just want you to know that you can talk to me about it – let me help you'; or, 'I noticed all those scars on your arms. I think you must be self-harming ... I want to help you. If you feel you don't want to talk to me, I can organise it for you to speak to someone else.'

If your child doesn't open up, try to remember that you are expecting them to talk about a very distressing and emotive subject. Don't ask the child why they are self-harming because in all likelihood they will go on the defensive. Instead gently help them acknowledge that they have a problem and encourage them to accept support and possibly professional help. You can encourage them to talk by using the phrase 'self-harm'. If they see that it doesn't cause you to react and respond in a frightened way, that you are not afraid of the word, and ergo the concept, they may be able to open up.

If your child is resistant and denies that they self-harm or there is a problem, remember that as their parents you are responsible for their physical and psychological welfare. You are not betraying them by openly admitting that help is required. There is no such thing as confidentiality when a child is in danger. If they insist that they don't have a problem, then tell them that you would like this confirmed by an expert. Give your child a few options of where you will bring them. Without trying to make them feel guilty or obliged to see someone, ensure that your child is aware that their self-harm affects all of you, that their distress is your distress.

Involving the Rest of the Family

Now that you have addressed the fact that self-harm affects all of you, this would be a good opportunity to ask the child if they want the rest of the family to know. Involve the child in this decision: discuss what the reasons would be for letting the rest of the family know – what would you be achieving? Coming to a mutual decision about who is to know and how it needs to be said can be very empowering for your child and will give them a great sense of respect and control. If you both decide that the family will be informed, have literature ready to distribute, and discuss it in such a way that it is not alarming or dramatic. Calmly say, 'N. has been trying to deal with some difficult issues and has coped by self-harming'. It is also important to ask your child if they want to be present when the disclosure is made.

If some members of the family are negative about your child's behaviour, or indeed if people outside the family are critical and act as if your child's behaviour is almost contagious, try not to be defensive and angry about it. Their lack of knowledge is making them act suspiciously and their reaction could be driven by fear. In a gentle way, your child should know that others sometimes view young people who self-harm as scary and they are afraid that either the young person will harm someone else or harm themselves in front of other children. Your friends and relatives need to know that this is not the case.

What To Do Next
The most important gift you can give your child now is the gift of listening. They do not want to hear your opinion, advice or quick-fix solutions. Let them know that you understand that they must be feeling some very difficult emotions and must be very frightened. Whatever you do, do not demand that they stop self-harming. If you turn this into a power struggle, everybody loses. Your child may come up with some very clear arguments about why they want to continue self-harming. If the child says they will stop without putting up a fight, be aware that they could substitute one method of self-harm with another. Your child can't suddenly just stop because you have asked them to. You need to firstly provide them with the reasons why you think they behave like this and then counteract them with informed reasons as to why they should stop self-harming. The following are ways in which you might answer defensive reasoning from your child as to why they should be allowed continue with their behaviour.

'WHY SHOULD I STOP? IT ONLY AFFECTS ME!'
Highlight that when they hurt themselves it helps them for only a short period of time. And it doesn't affect

only them; it harms their relationship with their family and with their friends if and when they find out.

Ask the young person how they would feel if they had a child who self-harmed. More than likely they will say they wouldn't want their child to ever self-harm. Then ask them why is it not okay for others to self-harm but it's okay for them.

'No one knows I self-harm'

Point out to them that though they have kept it hidden for a long time, eventually people will find out. As the need to harm increases, so does the severity of the wounds and telltale signs will become more obvious.

Ask your child how they would feel if their best friend, their cousin or Johnny down the road found out. Sometimes thinking about the shame or embarrassment a person who self-harms feels may be enough of a motive to seek help. Secrecy is an important part of self-harm because the person feels so ashamed of it.

'At least I know that people care about me and any attention is better than none'

Your child feels invisible. It could be for a very good reason. Perhaps they were overlooked – is there another child in the family who is ill or a parent with an addiction problem?

The child needs to know that from now on they won't be invisible; that they don't have to harm any more because they will be cherished and listened to.

They are confused by the word 'care' – explain to them that it's caring about someone that's important, not taking care of someone. Your child feels the need to be rescued, which gives way to feelings of abandon-ment if they feel they are not rescued.

'I AM A BAD DAUGHTER/SON'
All people who self-harm have a distorted view of their own character. Their self-hatred allows them to think the most terrible things about themselves. The mis-demeanours or 'sins' are often over-exaggerated and out of proportion. This is usually a result of the person believing that one or both parents do not love them. They need to be helped to come to the realisation that this is not the truth of the matter, and that you are there for them regardless.

'SELF-HARM PREVENTS ME FROM TAKING MY LIFE'
The reason they may believe that self-harming works is because they don't know of any other way of coping at this moment in time. It is possible to learn new coping methods, to gain the tools required to handle overwhelming emotions. At Pieta House, we would never tell a person to stop harming themselves and leave them with no coping tool. As a parent you must never tell a child to stop, or inspect their wounds to 'check up' on them. Never show disgust or disappoint-ment if they at any time revert back to self-harming.

'JUST THINKING OF STOPPING MAKES ME WANT TO DO IT MORE'
This is a very common feeling and, indeed, in Pieta House we find that for many young people the incidence of self-harm increases at the beginning. This is because their anxiety levels are sky high and they are afraid that they won't be able to cope. Try to remember that they

are hurting themselves for more reasons than before. It is no longer just an effective short-term source of relief.

These are just some of the arguments or reactions that you may have to face during the early stages of discovery or disclosure. Don't spend hours talking about it; take it slowly and at your child's pace. Your role at this stage is to plant seeds of doubt – in other words, that this behaviour is not useful – and also to plant seeds of love and acceptance.

Your child's worst fear has just been realised – they have been found out. They will now watch out for the slightest hint of rejection. Remember, the behaviour was hidden because of the shame and disgust your child feels about themselves.

Your reaction to your child after disclosure is important. If you go softly, softly, afraid to say a word in case you make them self-harm again, eventually you will be full of resentment and you will swiftly turn them into a victim. You will be creating an environment that is false, so your child will remain in a place where difficult situations are avoided. You still need to parent your child; they still need boundaries and directives.

While you are providing a supportive and validating environment, it is important that you get help for your child, and more importantly the right help. The following key points and attitudes have proven helpful in the aftermath of discovery:

- When someone listens, and is caring and accepting of the young person.
- Therapy that provides crisis support and strategies to reduce self-harm.

- Support groups.
- Families, especially a key member in the family who will provide support at home.

Exploring Therapy For Your Child

During this chaotic time, your own feelings are probably overwhelming. Anger, frustration and an enormous amount of fear are the natural, normal reactions upon discovery. Remind yourself that your child is in a great deal of emotional pain and about to commence a journey of learning how to voice that pain rather than act on it.

As parents, you cannot be expected to know how to deal with this problem alone. You too now need support and advice, as well as an outlet for your concerns and feelings. When going down the therapeutic route and trying to ascertain what might be the best course of action, it might be helpful to keep in mind the following regarding any counselling or therapy practice:

- That they have relevant experience and qualifications in dealing with people who self-harm.
- That there is a respectful and compassionate work ethos.
- That there is a clear understanding of the needs of someone who self-harms.
- That there is a realisation that self-harm is a coping strategy and not attention-seeking manipulation.
- That the therapists understand the difference between self-harm and suicide.

Don't be afraid to ask them how the therapy works: is it one-to-one or group therapy? It is our experience that one-to-one therapy works best for two very practical reasons: first, remember the behaviour is a hidden, secret one and it may be torturous for your child to have to speak publicly about it; second, there is the worry that group therapy for people who self-harm could become a forum for swapping war stories.

When discussing how the therapy works, ask them what model they follow: does it depend on the individual therapist, on their own skills, or is there a theoretical model that all the therapists work from? It is our opinion that there should be just one model that all therapists work from – that way it is easier to see if a part of it does not work. Also, many therapists have varying opinions on whether a 'No Harm Contract' should be put in place or if they work from a 'Harm Minimisation' perspective. Some therapists may also follow a 'Reward/Punishment' model. These models are explained below.

No Harm Contract
This is a written document between the therapist and the client – your child. It usually states that the therapist wants the young person not to harm themselves during the weeks or months they will be attending. It usually also states that if they do, either the contract will be terminated, or the young person needs to consider their commitment and make another appointment when they are ready.

We feel that this type of controlling pressure places the child under an enormous amount of stress. The therapist is asking the child to stop harming without putting any other coping tool in its place and the adaptation of a new coping skill will take time. Further, if the child does harm themselves during the next few weeks, not only is it the possible end of the relationship, but it means that after the child has gone through the agonies of disclosing their 'shameful' secret, they now feel more ashamed for relapsing, and they may have to wait a long time before they can go back to the therapist; even worse, they may have to disclose this secret to another therapist, another complete stranger.

Harm Minimisation

Harm minimisation or harm reduction is an approach that believes the following:

- Self-harm will continue to be part of our society.
- The removal and eradication of self-harm is impossible.
- Continued efforts at eradicating self-harm will only increase the behaviour in our society.

The aim of harm minimisation/reduction is to identify the individuals who participate in self-harm and implement strategies that will endeavour to minimise these harming behaviours. It is believed that this will be achieved by creating an environment that aims to assist people who self-harm in the safest manner by, for example:

- Providing clean blades for people who harm themselves by cutting.
- Educating people on the areas where it is safe to cut.

- Providing bandages and other medical equipment and teaching people how to tend to their wounds.
- Teaching these people other techniques, such as the use of elastic bands and ice cubes on the skin, which will provide pain but are less harmful.

Again, this is a practice that many therapists feel is useful without realising the impact it has on their clients. We at Pieta House do not agree with this form of therapy.

Most people who self-harm, as well as many therapists and clinicians, are aware of and armed with substitute strategies as alternatives or 'cures' for self-harming behaviours. These substitute strategies are a bit like chewing nicotine gum instead of smoking cigarettes – you are still receiving the nicotine even though you are not inhaling the harmful tar.

Harm minimisation is 'doing the action without the pain'. For example, some therapists will advise their patients to break eggs on their arms or thighs in order to create the sensation of warm blood flowing over the skin. Others will suggest immersing a limb in ice-cold water or holding an ice cube: the sharpness of the cold will seemingly bring the person back from an episode of dissociation. The same reasoning is behind the snapping of a rubber band against the wrist whenever there is an urge to self-harm, or using red markers to draw long thin lines down the arm or across the thighs to resemble cuts.

Many young people have been instructed to take up kickboxing or karate, or when the urge comes on them to self-harm, they have been advised to punch pillows or go into a room and 'let it all out' by screaming. While in theory this seems like good advice and is, after all, minimising the physical harm, there are serious problems with this approach and dangers even in these somewhat innocuous and innocent tactics. Karate and kickboxing almost entice the person into the path of their opponent's blows, which is more or less continuing self-harm. Drawing on the limbs with a red marker may have a cathartic effect, but while for many this type of approach may provide temporary relief, the problem is that when issues become more difficult or when further difficulties appear, these alternatives may not be enough.

The theory behind punching a cushion, for example, to release anger is that if it is not released, then the person is in danger of holding on to these negative states, which can turn toxic. People (and some therapists) believe that if these emotions are not released then they are 'just going to burst' and so we are encouraged to 'let off steam'. Using cathartic techniques and strategies, whatever they are, strengthens the belief that a young person must find a physical action to expel whatever strong emotion they are experiencing.

Cathartic methods can have many problems, however. Many of the strategies, for example, are not age appropriate or time appropriate. If your child is in the middle of class, they can't suddenly whip out a punching bag or do some kickboxing moves on the student sitting beside them. By providing these substitute tools and promoting them, we are reinforcing, over and over again, that strong emotions must be acted on. And like with the example of chewing nicotine gum instead of smoking cigarettes, the underlying problem is still there – the addiction to nicotine. Using substitute tools instead of self-harming is not dealing with the issue, or with the fact that we should not want to harm ourselves.

REWARD/PUNISHMENT

We have come across this method of reward and punishment not only in private practice but also in hospitals.

In our experience, punishment is the least effective way of controlling self-harming behaviours. Besides the fact that it doesn't work, it is also objectionable from a moral and ethical perspective. Using this method on people who are particularly sensitive to disapproval or blame gives them the message that the world out there is also harsh and punishing. Punishment can powerfully reinforce their feelings of worthlessness, shame and low self-esteem, which are the main emotions and states of mind that cause a person to self-harm in the first place. For some young people who see themselves as bad, evil or dirty, self-harm is a way of punishing themselves, so when a therapist/clinician applies punishment, it reinforces their opinion that they are dirty and bad.

Therapy must be about teaching children to verbalise emotions, not act on them. We need to let them know that emotions do not harm or kill you, but actions can. We need to help them understand that their bodies do not have to be a noticeboard indicating or highlighting the emotions they feel. We need to show them what the alternatives are.

Being informed and aware aids the healing journey. At that stage you can hand over the control of your child's recovery to the professionals.

Conclusion
The Pieta Way

PIETA HOUSE MISSION STATEMENT
To help hurting people walk through their times of pain and difficulty. To provide a holistic solution to the ever-increasing problems of hopelessness, despair and depression.

We in Pieta House believe that therapy, like medicine, should be specialised, and this is why we specifically focus on the two areas of suicide and self-harm. It is our hope that some day we will have a Pieta House in every county of Ireland, and that this will not only reduce suicide rates in our country, but also help people who self-harm turn to a different way of coping. If only we could help the child in early adolescence, we would be avoiding sometimes up to twenty or thirty years of self-harm. But in the meantime, we need to send a message out there to all the children and older people who self-harm that self-harm doesn't work! There are other ways of coping with difficult emotions.

At Pieta House we receive emails from all over the world – Pakistan, Zimbabwe, America, England and many parts of Europe – mainly asking, 'Where is the nearest Pieta House?' It was very simple to create Pieta House; all I had to do was think of what I would like to see and how I would like to be treated if I was in distress. I thought the best approach was to have a house that seemed welcoming and warm; an informal, non-clinical setting where people are greeted by name at the hall door, made feel welcome and provided with refreshments.

At the first meeting an assessment is carried out, which takes place in a warm living room where candles are lit and there is a great sense of tranquillity and calmness. The client sits on the couch and the assessor sits in front of them on a footstool, which means the person is seated higher than the assessor, symbolically representing the fact that they are in a position of control and will not be spoken down to. The meeting usually takes about thirty minutes to one hour and during that time we find out: how high-risk they are; if they are suicidal; or if they self-harm, how often they self-harm, how long they have been harming them-selves and, if possible, what reasons are behind the self-harm. The person is then assigned to a therapist – and then the real work gets started.

This is what I feel is the ideal scenario. But what about young people and children – what do they want, what are their needs? The answer is, their needs are exactly the same as adults. They want a warm, informal, non-clinical place; a place that will treat them with the utmost respect and kindness, that will not judge them or correct them, that will guide them to move away from self-harming behaviours, replacing them with coping tools and, more importantly, with dignity.

In standard psychiatric or psychotherapeutic practice, treatments tend to focus on the act of the injury itself, the dangers involved and the damage it does to the person and their families. Because of ignorance and misconceptions, some clinicians view self-harm as a behaviour that is random and chaotic; they miss the point that self-harm has complex and hidden meanings for the person who engages in it – if it didn't make sense, why would they continue to harm themselves?

Because of this lack of understanding, people regress, and indeed sometimes the self-harm increases, which reinforces the doctor's/therapist's view that self-harm is persistent and incurable. There is great danger when young people are hospitalised; so many messages are being sent here: that the child is 'sick', that they need to be restrained and, if it is a psychiatric hospital, that they are crazy. The danger, too, lies in the environment of the hospital, where contagion takes place: patients swapping methods, personal horror stories, comparing wounds and, worse still, competing for attention from the staff, which could cause dramatic and possibly life-threatening acts of self-cutting.

Although we may not agree with many other approaches, out of great respect to psychiatry and the people who work in the area, they make heroic efforts to keep their patients safe. When a person continues to self-harm, they do not realise the effect they have on the staff, who are also feeling helpless, hopeless and frustrated, because people who self-harm often sabotage their endeavours to create and maintain a relationship that is supportive and engaging.

However, what all nurses, doctors, clinicians and therapists need to realise is that by focusing on the harm – the action – you are becoming a character in the drama of the person's self-harm: you are becoming the rescuer. They must realise – and you, the parent, must also realise – that there is no such person who can keep the young person safe. With support and great patience, they must take responsibility themselves: they must keep themselves safe.

Importance of Relationship Between Therapist and Client

In Pieta House, we place great emphasis and importance on the relationship between the young person and the therapist. This crucial engagement, if successful, will be the turning point in your child's recovery. We inform young people from the beginning that if they feel they have not connected with the therapist after approximately two sessions, for whatever reason (for example, the therapist might remind them of someone), then we will provide them with another therapist. This is a very powerful and empowering action. It shows great respect to the young person; it involves them and reinforces how important a supportive relationship is, one that they may not have had before. This relationship is not a mothering or parental relationship, but a relationship that works in collaboration with the young person so that they can discover together what emotions and difficulties are behind the self-harming behaviours.

Our therapeutic response to self-harm is a model we have created that is specifically designed to bring the person from self-harm to self-care. Each therapist lives by standard rules and procedures during the therapeutic relationship. These include:

- Creating a relationship that establishes rapport and trust, and that at all times demonstrates compassion and kindness, because that is what Pieta House has been built on.
- In an authentic way, building the self-esteem and acknowledging the positive characteristics in the young person. This will entail making them aware, possibly for the first time, of their attributes and strengths, while at the same time building their confidence about past achievements and triumphs.
- Never asking a young person to stop self-harming, because to do so establishes the therapist as the one in control, not the young person. Self-harm has to cease because the child wants it to stop.
- Never showing disappointment or being disappointed if the young person who has stopped self-harming relapses; such a reaction indicates that the agenda has become the therapist's, not the child's. The therapist believes that if a young person relapsed it was because they were so overwhelmed at the time and could not remember any other alternative. The therapist is aware that self-harm may increase at the beginning of therapy because of the anxiety levels of the young person, coupled with the fear of stopping.
- Discovering the triggers and the underlying emotions that cause the young person to self-harm. The triggers could be conflict in the home,

either between parent and child or siblings or parents. Further triggers could be the breakdown of relationships within the school setting or pressure on academic performance. Feelings of not fitting in and isolation could also be triggers. The therapist will provide the young person with a daily record sheet that will track and map the activities and emotions of their day. This is an essential tool in the therapeutic process. It teaches the young person not only to identify their triggers, but also to name the emotion that is evoked from that trigger. This record sheet will allow the therapist and the young person to work in collaboration and will avoid all attitudes or expectations of the therapist 'curing' the client.

- The therapist and the young person, together, will now come up with alternative ways of coping with their difficulties and emotions. It is essential that these alternatives be chosen by the child rather than by the therapist, because what might work for one person may not work for another. These alternatives also include the methods the young person used on the occasions when they didn't self-harm. Including these alternatives gives the young person that very strong belief that they have coped in a safe way before, that action does not always have to follow emotion and that self-harm does not have to be a way of life.

- The subsequent meetings between the therapist and the young person will be about tracking, testing and perfecting. Tracking and mapping the emotions must continue because it teaches them to verbalise the emotion or difficulty. The testing is where new alternatives are tried out to see if they work. The perfecting is where, on discovering the coping tools that do work, these tools are honed and refined so that they become an automatic response to emotional or difficult situations.

- As the therapy is coming to an end, there is no way of knowing how long the work will last for. It is entirely dependent on the young person, their motivation, their desire to stop the behaviour and, most importantly, the relationship between the therapist and the child. But this crucial stage must accomplish two objectives. First, it must predict scenarios that could pose potential distress and emotional pain, and then go through that with the young person, visualising how they would handle it. This is essential because the therapist and the young person would have been mainly focusing on past and present emotions and difficulties until now, but the child needs to know that they can handle any future highly emotive situation without resorting to self-harm. The second objective is, with the young person's permission and collaboration, to switch support and care from the therapist to another key person – this person could be a family member or another adult who is willing to continue the support. It is hoped that there will be no difficulty in this, because part of the therapist's aim is to make this young person independent, capable and secure in the knowledge that therapy does not continue forever and that they are now capable of forming solid relationships that are based on mutual trust and friendship.

- If the child is very young and unable to track and map their emotions and difficulties, we adapt the therapy around them. Our therapists are trained in child therapy through play, and while this offers ways of communicating and demonstrating their distress through objects, we have discovered that all the children who come to Pieta House are able to engage in dialogue, sometimes in a very mature fashion. We also engage with a member of the child's family, who will complete the daily activity sheet for the child. This will enable the therapist to see what daily activities or situations evoke strong emotions in the child. Of course, the family person who will be assisting the therapist will, at first, have the sole role of gathering data or information; later, they will be a key figure in taking over the supportive role of the therapist. We have discovered that the younger the child is, the easier it is to move them away from self-harming behaviours to verbalising their feelings.

One of the goals of our therapy is to try to show each person, whether adult or child, that they have at their disposal the skills to stop self-harming and control how they react to difficult events in their life, but these skills must be cultivated. Another goal is to get them to firmly realise that not every single emotion or feeling has to be reacted to with physical action. This goal will inevitably teach the young person that it is not necessary to respond to urges; that these urges do not need to be immediately gratified; that they need to slow down, think and reflect on what they could do instead.

In Pieta House, we do not view abstinence from self-harm as a cure or, indeed, as a successful therapeutic outcome. Although our ultimate goal is to move the young person from self-harm to self-care, we believe that success should be measured by their experience – being accepted, valued, respected, having their experiences validated and understood and knowing that they deserve to have their needs met and to engage in self-care as opposed to self-harm. This comprehensive therapy will help all people who self-harm, young or old, to stop harming behaviours and learn more successful coping strategies.

We aim to train therapists or people working on the front line with marginalised groups – such as people who have addiction problems, the travelling community, people who are incarcerated, people who work with young people in adolescent psychiatric units – in the Pieta Way. This will mean that everyone in Ireland will be able to access help when in crisis and will be truly, compassionately accompanied during their difficult journey.

I am sure there are many other dedicated organisations and therapists that also offer help to those who self-harm. Their compassion and respect for their client will help them more than anything else. Studies have shown how compassion is probably the key to helping people change their life and their behaviours forever (Rein, Atkinson and McCraty, 1995). For more information on counselling or support in or near your locality, contact www.hse.ie or telephone 1850 241850.

We have seen in Pieta House that kindness alone can move a person to want to change. We have seen that holding a person's hand and showing sincere affection (as opposed to 'group hug' situations) can move mountains – the mountains being the behaviours or the agonies that people, and young people in particular, have to overcome. We as a country, a society, a community, need to overcome the urge to judge, and instead look at the person who is dealing with difficult issues with compassion, respect and total acceptance. Then we will be in a position to reduce the numbers of people who are suicidal, and support, nurture and verbally caress the people – in particular our children – who self-harm.

Appendix
About Pieta House

Pieta House is based in Lucan, Co. Dublin. It looks like a very ordinary house from the outside, just like all the houses beside it. Yet once you arrive at the hall door there is a powerful sense of tranquillity. You are greeted by name, and the joke is that, whether you want it or not, you are given a cup of tea the moment you sit down in the sunroom. After an assessment, the client is then assigned to a therapist and that's when the real work begins. Our job is not to focus on the past: although we will hear the person's story, we will not linger on, ruminate over or analyse why the person's life has unravelled. We are here to lift suicidal ideation or self-harming behaviour and replace the reasons for dying or harming with reasons for living with dignity. We will become that person's energy; we will look at their life in the present and project them into the future.

This can be a new beginning for the client, a time for them to see what is really important in their lives. Through one-to-one therapy, an important relationship will develop between two people: the therapist and the client. When we speak about topics concerning life and death, a very intimate and personal rapport is built up between therapist and client.

If this relationship is right, the client will respond to the compassion and care that is being offered, and the therapist will encourage them and provide alternative strategies that the client can implement in their lives. For many, and perhaps for the first time, they realise that there may be solutions to their problems.

During the last four years, we have had to make some tough decisions. Because our therapy is 'talking therapy', it means that the client must be able to engage in conversation. People who rely heavily on drugs or alcohol would not find our type of therapy beneficial because studies show that people make rash and impulsive decisions when they are taking such substances. Studies have shown that people who are distressed and are heavy drinkers are six times more likely to attempt suicide than those who do not drink (Self-Harm Registry, Western HSC, Northern Ireland, 2007/2008).

Because our therapy is about dialogue, it may not be suitable for people who are intellectually challenged or who have a serious psychiatric disorder that makes them view the world in an irrational and chaotic way. However, it is important that these people are neither forgotten about nor censored, so we have created a workshop to provide training for therapists/carers who work with marginalised groups to equip them to help people who are suicidal or who self-harm.

PIETA HOUSE
OLD LUCAN ROAD
LUCAN, CO. DUBLIN
T. 01 601 0000
W. WWW.PIETA.IE

Bibliography

Bowlby, J., *Maternal Care and Mental Health*, Schocken, 1951.

Diagnostic and Statistical Manual of Mental Disorders (DSM-IV-TR) (4th ed.), American Psychiatric Association, 2000.

Mosby's Medical, Nursing, and Allied Health Dictionary (4th ed.), Kenneth N. Anderson (ed.), C.V. Mosby, 1994.

ARTICLES/SURVEYS
'Choosing Mental Health: A Policy Agenda for Mental Health and Public Health', Mental Health Foundation, 2005.

Gardner, D.L., Cowdry, R.W. 'Alprazolam-Induced Dyscontrol in Borderline Personality Disorder', *American Journal of Psychiatry*, 1985.

Meltzer, H., Corbin, T., Gatward, R., Goodman, R., Ford, T., 'The Mental Health of Young People Looked

After by Local Authorities in England', The Office for National Statistics, 2002.

Platt, S., Bille-Brahe, A., Kerkhof, A. et al., 'Parasuicide in Europe: the WHO/EURO Multicentre Study on Parasuicide', *Acta Psychiatrica Scandinavica*, 1992.

Rein, G., Atkinson, M., McCraty, R., 'The Physiological and Psychological Effects of Compassion and Anger', *Journal of Advancement in Medicine*, 1995.

Samaritans and Centre for Suicide Research, University of Oxford, 2002.

'Scientific and Social Value Judgements', National Institute for Health and Clinical Excellence, 2004: www.nice.org.uk/pdf/boardmeeting/ brdmay04item6.pdf (accessed 15 Jun 2004).

Soloff, P.H., Lis, J.A., Kelly, T., Cornelius, J., Ulrich, R., 'Risk Factors for Suicidal Behaviour in Borderline Personality Disorder', *American Journal of Psychiatry*, 1994.

Self-Harm Registry, Western HSC, Northern Ireland, 2007/2008.

Winchel, R.M., Stanley, M., 'Self-Injurious Behaviour: A Review of the Behaviour and Biology of Self-Mutilation', *American Journal of Psychiatry*, 1991.